HELLO AGAIN —
ANOTHER MONDAY
MORNING

John Jackson

LAKELAND
MARSHALL MORGAN & SCOTT
116 Baker Street,
LONDON W1M 2BB

Copyright © John Jackson 1975
First published 1975

ISBN 0 551 00558 0

Made and printed in Great Britain by
Hunt Barnard Printing Ltd., Aylesbury, Bucks.

This book is dedicated with fondest love to Stuart and Helen, Irene and Barrie, ours and theirs —now all ours.

CONTENTS

FOREWORD

People who can write books are lucky. So are people who can read them. But the luckiest are the people who can understand books and gain the message the writer gives.

John Jackson's books are a knockout. If you can really capture his quite simple message it will improve your life. Maybe only a little, but perhaps a lot.

What more could a book ask of you – or you of the book?

God bless.

JIMMY SAVILE, OBE

PREFACE

If somebody asked me to write down briefly what I have seen, over many years now, to have been my job as a Methodist minister, I should be hard pressed to choose between two statements. To solve that dilemma let me declare them both. Here they are:

1. To comfort the afflicted and to afflict the comfortable.
2. To speak a good word for Jesus.

That is what I have tried to do in all my broadcasts and some of them are published here only because so many folk have asked for this second book. I am grateful to all these and indeed also to many others who have been kind enough to write to me over the years.

Again my wife has helped me, especially in reading the proofs – thereby adding to those very many things she does for me all the time.

I want to thank Jimmy Savile OBE for his Foreword, so typical and readily given, and also for his friendship – so genuine.

To Miss Rosalie Poole, my secretary, I am indebted for all the typing – once she's read my writing! – always done without complaint and always there on time.

Father Pat McEndoe of the BBC is far more than a fine producer. He is a man of God – and this shows. I owe him so much.

Finally, a thank you to my publishers for their continued guidance, patience and encouragement.

JOHN JACKSON
Whitechapel Methodist Mission, 1974

DOMINOES

Hello again on another Monday morning!

I went back recently to the small Cheshire town where I was born and grew up and I've been walking down memory lane. We didn't boast of a park but we did have a recreation ground – always referred to as 'the Rec'. In the holidays we used to play there – cricket and football in due season. No referees or umpires, and the number on either side was simply half the number of those who had turned up. On wet days we'd hang around in a kind of pagoda pavilion, or, greatly daring, we would go and peep through the windows of the old men's hut – a sort of senior citizens' club. Inside, round a coke stove usually red hot, sat these old men – they looked ninety or a hundred to us lads and the air was thick with smoke from coke and thick twist tobacco. At odd times they might let one or two of us in and we watched them in dead silence through the smoke, playing dominoes, more intent than Eisenhower planning the invasion of Europe or Peter Scott bird watching. The only noise was the click of the dominoes – or a knock on the table when somebody couldn't go or else the triumphant word 'CHIPS' as someone played their last domino and in so doing had won the game. A noise for a minute or two while those remaining in the losers' hands were recorded, and then another pensive, silent battle began.

Well, recalling that reminded me of something rather curious that Jesus once said. It was this: 'Whoever seeks to gain his life shall lose it, but whoever loses his life shall save it.'

The reason those strange words came to my mind was this. Have you ever really noticed that you only win at dominoes when you've lost them all; when they are all on the table, you've got rid of them and hold none in your hand? The more you hold and keep in your hand, the further you are from victory when the final score is added up. You gain by losing – you win by emptying.

We're getting very near to the centre of things that really matter here – near to the truth about Jesus dying on a cross. God GAVE His only begotten Son to die on the Cross. Nothing left – all given to die. It was because God gave like that, that He won. You see, the Cross was a battle between God and the Devil, Good and Evil – and Bad Friday became Good Friday because Jesus rose from the dead and He has beaten sin and death once and for all. But it only happened because God gave ALL.

This, as I have said so often, is an age of grasping and getting, gaining and grabbing – setting store by what we possess, what we hold and what we own and call ours. Jesus says, 'No – it's like dominoes. If you want to preserve, to keep – you must give away; you must lose. If you want to win – then let go and lose hold.'

Even though it was only a game of dominoes, I seem to recall that when they did win, those old men, there was a smile on their faces and a light of victory in their eyes.

Well, who cares about going CHIPS at dominoes – it matters little. It does matter, though, if there is a smile on your face and a light of victory in your eyes; and there could be if you would lose yourself and find Jesus Christ as your Saviour and Lord.

So a prayer to end:

Teach us Lord Jesus, that what we keep never has any future and that what we give to you lasts for ever.

AMEN

PASSING THE BUCK

It's not a very elegant way of expressing things but my goodness it makes things quite plain, and because of that I like it. I've not gone much for folk who speak chocolate éclair and bay window – I prefer bread and cheese and honest homespun language. So, though it be not elegant, I know what someone means when they talk to me about 'passing the buck'.

I think it's worth a thought if only for the reason that it is such an age-old way of doing things. Do you know, they were doing it in the Garden of Eden; it's not me it's the woman, it's not me it's the man, it's not us it's the serpent. Yes, they were at it as long ago as that. Yet it's plain to see it wasn't the apple on the tree where the trouble began. No, it was the pair on the ground.

Every day of every week I have, to a greater or lesser degree, something to do with men and women whose lives are a mess and a misery. Scores who come to us are homeless and hopeless, ill-fed, ill-clad, dirty and dejected, and in so very many cases initially (and notice I said initially) they all blame something or somebody else. The home, the family, the wife, husband, boss, the drink, the horses, they, them, always initially the others. Rarely, all too rarely, do they begin in the right place.

This is not only true of those who come to our Mission, but in maybe more sophisticated ways it's also too true of so many of us. I know it's quite often true of me. I can cover, I can explain, I can excuse all my faults and failures by passing the buck and I find that sometimes I do it so convincingly that I even manage to convince myself. I don't speed – I had to overtake; the fellow in front was all over the road. I don't lose my patience – the woman was beyond reasonable human endurance. I'm not thoughtless – my work does really make me preoccupied quite often. I'm not overweight and needing to diet – I'm just not as tall as I should be for someone my weight. That may sound good to you this Monday

11

morning unless you happen to know I'm six foot two!

Well, if you are still with me and have not passed the buck and felt that all I'm saying is for someone else, indeed anybody else but you, let me say it now very simply before I finish.

I don't think that it is altogether a coincidence that the middle letter of the word SIN is the letter I. I also know when I'm quite honest with myself that for me and for you and for every man, Public Enemy Number One – IS Number One.

This is why I'm so glad that there are personal pronouns at the very heart of my Faith, so glad in the knowledge that Jesus died for ME and that He is MY Saviour, so glad that He and He alone can and does deal with the SIN in my life so that there is never any need for me to go on passing the buck. All I need to do is to let Him come into my life as Saviour and Lord and all that is wrong is dealt with by His greatness and love.

A prayer now:

Forgive us for placing blame for our sins in the wrong places. Let us see ourselves for what we are and then through the love of Jesus become the people whom we could and should be. Through Jesus Christ our Lord.

AMEN

HELEN'S DAY

The weekend just passed has been a very special one for me, a sort of milestone in my life. You see, I have only one daughter and she got married on Saturday.

All the usual things have been said about me not losing a daughter, but rather finding a son. I'm sure that's true and I seem to remember someone in similar circumstances telling me he lost a daughter and found a bathroom. Well, there may be a lot in that too, but let's get back to weddings for a moment.

We all speak about the happy couple, made for each other, two people joined together as one for life, and all that is true in any real Christian marriage. The emphasis is upon two people, 'this man and this woman', the bride and bridegroom. In fact they are emphasised so much that I sometimes think something very important is forgotten, overlooked or lost in confetti, cake and catering; smothered, or maybe even drowned, in all the trimmings that are so often a major part of a wedding these days.

If anything happens to either husband or wife, some tragedy, some accident, some break up, everyone who knows them and loves them is really distressed and upset. Again it's very right that it should be so, but still the emphasis is upon the two, the man and wife, the couple.

Let me remind you, in case you've forgotten or lest it has never really struck you, that any real wedding in a Christian church begins like this: 'Dearly beloved we are gathered together *in the sight of God*', and so on. So a wedding is not just something about two people and their future life together. There are three involved and the third person is God; God as we know Him in Jesus Christ.

Folk have wished my daughter and her new husband 'Good luck'. I sincerely hope they're not relying on that because there 'ain't no such thing'.

Others have wished for them prosperity and good health. I hope they have their fair share of both, but I know from my own experience neither of those are much to be depended upon as the years come and go.

No, what I wish for them, and for all of you who were married in church, is that they'll go on as they began, in the presence of God. I hope they will always keep a place for Jesus in their hearts and in their homes. Then they need never bother about luck, and wealth and health may be theirs or not, but their love for each other will grow, and so will yours, as the days go by.

And now a prayer:

We thank you, O Lord, for Christian marriage and for Christian homes. Help us to realise that our nation can only be truly great if it is built on the foundations of such hearth-stones. Through Jesus Christ our Lord.

AMEN

QED

I think I was just above average at mathematics at school – I can still remember Pythagoras and in none of my churches as yet has there ever been a collection I couldn't count. Well, it's good to know a bit about maths these days because everyday somebody is telling us about percentages relating to the cost of living – yes, and dying, the swing in voting, the Value Added Tax, the threshold, the wages claim, the gross this and the net that. All very complicated and yet, as I say, figuring large in our lives today.

I was turning over in my mind the other day what the Bible has to say about mathematics, where it mentions figures and numbers. It was worth more than a glance, I'll tell you.

Once, in those schooldays I mentioned a moment or two ago, I got a 99 per cent in a Latin examination. I and everyone else was completely satisfied – you don't get many 99's never mind a 100, do you? Yet the Bible says that 99 per cent isn't enough for God. If ninety-nine of His hundred children are safe and sound – all except ONE – then at any cost He goes out to seek that one and He goes on searching until He finds; and you know this is very important indeed if that ONE happens to be you or me.

Here's another bit of Bible maths. Every now and then when someone wrongs me, I've discovered I can forgive them and I've even managed to do so when they've done it once or twice more! But when they go on, I find myself saying, 'Here come off it, enough of this. What do you take me for? You've had your last chance. Away you go and find some other sucker.' To forgive folk six or seven times is asking a bit much. Yet the Bible says I've got to go on forgiving until seventy times seven.

Both of my parents came from large families, so I had a lot of relatives and I knew them all. I also knew everybody in the whole of two streets where I used to live and that adds up to a lot of folk. But the Bible says God knows ME and YOU – as though every hair on our heads was numbered. And He knows sparrows too.

The Bible says you can tell who the real followers of Jesus are by mathematics. If someone wants a lift for a mile a lot of folk might help but true Christians will go twice as far as that. If somebody feels cold a few folk would find them a jacket but true Christians throw in an overcoat as well. The Bible says God treats us not just with kindness or even love but that He adds them together and treats us with loving kindness. The little boy said when his Mum gave him a piece of bread and butter that was kindness but when she put jam on it that was loving kindness and I think that boy got his sum right.

St Paul got himself tied up a bit when he tried to put the Bible mathematics into words. He wrote, 'God is able to do exceeding abundantly above anything we can ask or think.' There was no number big enough.

Does your life add up all right this morning, have you figured out what real Christianity is all about? There may not be any four figure tables to help but there is a four letter word – LOVE.

Now a prayer:

Lord Jesus, who counted a crown of thorns to be of bigger value than a crown and throne in heaven, help us to see in that your incalculable love. Add more of your grace to our lives and take away everything that is unlike you. Make us to be numbered among all those who are fit to bear your name.

AMEN

A DEAD CERT!

When I was a lad nobody seemed to fear talking about death but not a word was mentioned about sex. Nowadays everybody talks – ad nauseam – about sex and very few folk want to talk about death. I would go further, they'll go to amazing lengths to avoid using the word. They speak of passing on and passing over, departing, falling on sleep and relinquishing this mortal coil – or toil – anyhow, something like that; anything but death and dying.

Admittedly though, when I come to think about it, our forefathers did use what now seems strange language to talk about death, but it wasn't strange to them. It was Bible, Scripture-based, and since this was familiar language to them they spoke in that way. We who are not so familiar with the Bible do, as I say, find it strange. One of their favourite ways of speaking about death was to refer to it as 'crossing over Jordan'. They used this picture language because they knew that the children of God – His chosen ones – had done just that. Delivered by God they had been guided by Him across the River Jordan to their destination, their Promised Land. So my grandparents believed they were God's chosen and God's children and that He would lead them across death – Jordan – to their land which He had promised, that place called heaven. They sang about standing on the brink of Jordan and not shrinking, of being unafraid because of the promises of Jesus.

A very dear friend of mine was taken seriously ill some months ago and he knew for a time that his life hung in the balance. Writing to me and speaking to me afterwards he said, 'My goodness, John, I've often sung about "treading the verge of Jordan", but by gum I felt so close the soles of my feet were wet.'

You know, according to an old workmate of mine on the railway – a man named Charlie Hill – there are only two things in life you can be sure of. These are those two things Charlie told me about nearly forty years ago:

17

(1) The rent man will call every week.

(2) Death, that's a cert.

He's not far off the truth in that, is he? Sooner or later, in God's good time – not ours – we all arrive there.

What then? Have you thought about that or are you afraid to think or talk about death? Let me tell you a little, only a little but perhaps enough, of what I think.

When Columbus was sailing out west over uncharted seas, his crew, his sailors, grew more and more afraid. They believed the world was flat, that they would sail over the edge and perish. But Columbus kept urging them on and crying over and over again, 'There's life beyond the sunset.'

Yes, that's what I believe. Why? Because Jesus has told me, and you if you'll believe Him. He's told me, 'Because I live you shall live also.' He does and I will.

A prayer:

Lord Jesus, keep me trusting in your promises now and into eternity.

AMEN

GLORY HOLE

When I was a lad at home we always referred to the cupboard under the stairs as the 'glory hole' – I've no idea why, it was always clean and always tidy. Under there those things were stored, at the back at any rate, which we rarely ever needed – Christmas decorations, old pictures, some brassware which used to be on the hearth, candles, bulb bowls out of season and suitcases. There's always something fascinating about going to a glory hole to find something; it often works out to be serendipity.

I was rooting about recently in the one we've got now, even though we've no stairs, the store place in which we keep things rarely used. I noticed right at the back two oldish and rather large suitcases we've never used since we were fortunate enough once to cross the Atlantic on the *Queen Elizabeth*. I noticed the shipping line labels and also labels which said 'not wanted on voyage' and that set me thinking. Thinking how easy and popular it is to get and to hold on to things on the voyage we call life which really we should have labelled 'not wanted on voyage' and thrown out long ago.

For a number of years we lived near to a very charming couple who had fled from one of the European countries just before the last war. I remembered the man telling me about it. He said there came a knock on his door quite late one night. It was a friend come to tell him to get out there and then. He'd about half an hour. After that it was the concentration camp and inevitably death. So he and his wife had to grab everything they wanted on the voyage as it were and flee for their lives. They left a fully furnished home and they've never seen it since. They took only what they could carry and at the same time travel and travel quickly.

I wonder what you and I would think was wanted on a voyage like that. Money really isn't much use, nor are the fridge and the television – not even if it's colour. You can't carry thickly piled carpets, nor can you transport décor and candelabra. I asked my friends what they took; perhaps I don't remember everything, but some things I do. They took two photographs of their grandchildren, she took a rosebud from the garden, they took a Bible and some old love letters and then he said, 'we took our memories'.

I'm wondering if I'm travelling light, if I'm not getting overloaded in these days. I'm wondering if it has caught up with me, this spirit of getting and having more and more things. It's good to pause for a moment, to see what we've got and what we're working for and running after and to ask quietly and solemnly, 'Is it really wanted on the voyage?'

It's easy to sing, 'I'd rather have Jesus than anything.' But if you can sing it and mean it then and only then can you be sure that your treasure and heart are in the right place. Then and only then can you be sure that you are sailing safe and not weighed down below the plimsoll line and in danger of shipwreck.

A prayer:

Grant, O God, to us a wise discernment, the ability to know what matters and the courage to seek only that in time and for eternity.

AMEN

NO FIXED ABODE

There used to be an old ditty that said something about packing up and going away all for the sake of a holiday. To do just that is sometimes something of a fag, we may think, but in the end as a rule we feel that it was well worth it. But then too there is the packing up when you are on holiday, the packing up and going home. It's traditional to moan about this, I suppose, and to make such comments as, 'All over for another year . . . back to the grindstone'. Yet even so for me there is always something wonderful about going home. Whenever I have been away, be it for a long time or a short time, I get a kick out of the very thought of going home.

This has always been so for me but much more so in recent years. The reason for this being that in these recent years I have met so many folk who have not got a home to go to; not anywhere on earth is there a place that they can call their home. I have heard them referred to as being ROOTLESS. They have got a name, some kind of clothes, they manage something to eat here and there, they have got a come-from but they have not got a go-to, no hearth, no home.

When scores of them wander off from my Mission on a nice warm August Sunday night I don't feel too badly about it, after all we have given them a bit of supper. But it's a different story on a rotten icy cold night in January with the sleet falling and the wind blowing. No home to go to, no bed, no warmth, no shelter, no roots.

For a parson to talk to you about God is a reasonably safe thing, but when I begin to talk about people and perhaps especially rootless, homeless people, it is far from simple and straightforward. Time and time again I have mentioned God wanting, and indeed God deserving, our love and very many of us believe in all sincerity that we do love Him. But we're back in trouble again when we talk about loving God, for as far as I know there is only one

21

possible way of demonstrating that we love God, and that is by our loving men.

This is what the Bible means when it talks about compassion, this is what Jesus did when the Bible says He showed compassion. He moved towards them with an outstretched hand. How is any man to know that we love him unless we do just that? Nothing alters at all when we merely tell a man that we love him. It only becomes fact, relevant, vital when love moves into action, which again is just what this thing called compassion is.

All that I have been saying so far is true of our relationship with every man. But a dictum that John Wesley gave to his followers was this, 'Don't just go to those who need you, but go to those who need you most.' Strong words and hard to follow, I know, but I believe that they are as much the teaching of Jesus as the words of Wesley. Isn't His story of the sheep and the goats a parable about the very things I have tried to emphasise here? There is still plenty of scope even in a Welfare State for all of us to find another somewhere who is in some kind of need; and there is always someone somewhere to whom and for whom we can be the love of God.

One man, on hearing of a case of real need, said to the man who told him about it, 'I'm sorry.'

'Yes,' the man replied, 'I'm sorry £5. How sorry are you?'

Well, how sorry are you?

Here's a prayer for this morning:

Let my heart ache for those in need and move me to action on their behalf that I also from time to time may have backache.

AMEN

22

SEWING OR REAPING!

Even in my days on the railway it was something you saw quite often at most wayside railway stations. My father used to tell me that in his day as a porter on the old LNWR it was something accepted as normal as selling and collecting tickets. There would arrive in the guard's compartment, along with parcels, mail bags, dogs, etc., baskets full of pigeons. The porter would carry them as a rule to the end of the platform and then he would release them. I've seen them circle the station two or three times and then fly off, north, south, east or west depending on where their home was. The porter would write the time of release on the basket, reverse the label, and the basket would be sent back to the home where it came from to rejoin the pigeons. Usually home was scores or even hundreds of miles away but, pigeons being pigeons, saving mishap, those amazing birds would fly back. They went home to roost, as the pigeon fanciers would say.

One great pigeon fancier named Kenty once said to my father after he had released his birds and they flew away out of sight, 'Look at them pigeons – out of sight Sam – aren't they grand uns?'

I was reminded of pigeons coming home to roost when I read an incident in a novel recently. I don't know how true it was but in any case it contains an eternal truth. A famous figure in the National life of this country over half a century ago got into trouble over financial matters, and this man, whose name was a household word, was convicted of the offences when he was charged and sent to prison. When he was in prison he was given the task of sewing mail bags. Someone visiting the prison saw him at this task and in passing commented, 'Ah, ah. Sewing.' He looked up very sadly and answered, 'No, reaping.'

I meet a lot of people almost every day who are doing just that. In many cases they are reaping what they have sown but also in some cases the sowing was not theirs but only the harvest. I suppose legally you could say to them,

'Well, serves you right, you've got your deserts; you made your bed, now you must lie on it,' and I suppose legally you would be right and also just. But I can't accept that as the last word, and I'll tell you why.

A very ugly woman with lots of money commissioned a great artist to paint her portrait. At every sitting she kept saying in a very haughty voice, 'My man, I trust you are doing me justice.' The artist stuck this for as long as he could and then one day he replied, 'Madam, it's not justice you need, it's mercy!'

That goes for me too and for you; and that's why I do what John Wesley did so often – I offer men Christ. My loving Lord is merciful and forgiving and it is of the character of His Father God always to have mercy. If I couldn't tell my friends in the East End that good news I'd pack it all in today.

A prayer now:

We thank you, Lord Jesus, that in your presence we are not only dealt with justly but also mercifully.

AMEN

TELEPHONE KIOSK

I've noted several times when my daughter has been telling someone how to get to her house she always says, 'You will easily find Plank's Lane off the village green. Keep on coming down the lane until you come to a telephone kiosk and turn left after that, and we're third house up on the left.' Sounds all so easy doesn't it? Well, I found it so the first time I went there down the lane, until there sure enough on the left was the traditional GPO telephone kiosk standing out and red, and there we were at our destination. If you were me you would have looked out for that red kiosk.

But a week or so ago I saw something I've never noticed before in all my life. I was told – I don't know how true it is – that it is the only one in London. Just off the Victoria Embankment in London there is a telephone kiosk the same shape and size as the thousands of others I've seen, but for some reason not known to me it is painted GREEN. I wonder why! It's the authentic thing and yet it looks so different from what we have grown to expect.

Years ago I visited that part of New York called China Town and there I was shown a telephone kiosk made to look like a pagoda.

I've seen too in an eating house near Bolton a telephone box which to all intents and purposes looks from the outside like a kind of sedan chair.

Yet in both these cases – pagoda and sedan chair – they are the authentic article and fulfil the same use as the standard red kiosk even though they are so different from what I would expect. Turn left at the telephone kiosk – red, of course, you take that for granted.

One of the saddest things to encounter is intolerance. Folk have certain fixed ideas on this or that and utterly refuse to accept that something or someone can be authentic, genuine, or real if it doesn't fit in with their preconceived concrete notions. You can't have a telephone kiosk if it isn't red, and that's that, full stop!

There are people who think like that about God and about Jesus. It is as if they had got them in a box – their box mind you, all neat and sealed up and no place for variations at all. Some think like that about the Church – their Church. Any other is pretence, sham, less than one hundred per cent. Some think like that about people who are trying to be Christians. They have got a kind of mental template and only when something or someone fits that pattern perfectly is it accepted as the genuine article. 'After all,' they would say, 'you can't have a telephone kiosk that isn't RED.'

I wish they, indeed I wish we all, would remember Jesus was rejected as genuine because He didn't conform in the eyes of either Church or State in His day, and that intolerance meant a Cross. I know He doesn't want any of us to be like that today. Jesus saw good in Zacchaeus and he was as far from the accepted norm as a green telephone kiosk.

We'll end with a prayer.

Prevent us, O Lord, from making hasty and wrong judgements because we see something or someone different from ourselves or our views.

AMEN

SCRAP VALUE

I've just had a few days' holiday in the Midlands chiefly in order to see my new granddaughter. She's a smasher, bless her. While up there I was able to see a few old acquaintances. One of them told me about a mutual friend who had a wrought-iron picture frame which had got broken, and how he went to a great deal of trouble to get it repaired. You know what happens, someone knew a chap who knew a chap whose wife's sister had married another chap who worked with a fellow who would do it!

It must have arrived at the right chap in the end and subsequently after many weeks it arrived back to its owner, restored and ready for use again. When he got it back he was preoccupied and he put it down and carried on with his work and went out. When he got back at night he went to get it and presumably to put a picture in it and hang it. It was gone. He then did what all husbands do, asked the wife where she had put it. 'Oh that,' she said, 'I've broken it up and put it in the dustbin – scrapped it.' I have no report of what he said, but perhaps since he was what is sometimes called a prominent Methodist layman he said, 'Oh dear me.' Anyhow, I gather it's now on its way towards its second phase of reconstruction, so let's hope all will be well this time.

Now to go back to my friend on whom I had called. He is a JP and he said, 'I suppose it doesn't matter much when it's only a picture frame, but all too often I sit in court and it isn't a picture frame that's scrapped, it's a marriage, a home, a career, a character and perhaps worst of all, the laughter of little children.'

These, my old friend told me – but this really I know and know only too well – these are regularly being treated as of little or no value and thrown on to the scrap heap. Nationally and internationally we have daily been confronted over recent months with this kind of news. It is happening in what are sometimes referred to as 'high' places as well as in the small-town magistrates' courts where my friend sits.

For me to be told that this is freedom, the spirit of the age, a broader way of life and the like, and that I'm old fashioned and do not keep up with the times, doesn't affect one little bit my own view that it's not any or all of these things so labelled. For me it is sad, wrong and sinful, and while I spend my life in trying to help the sinner I also condemn the sin, whenever and wherever it rears its ugly head.

A Monday morning is a good time for us all to consider just what is of value that we might be in danger of throwing into the dustbin. What is there in our lives that because of our way of life is on the way to being scrapped?

And last of all today – if you have done wrong and already you have thrown away through your own folly something or someone of real worth and value, well, it's never too late to start again with Jesus. His purpose in coming here was salvation, or if you like, salvage. Maybe you need Him to do just that for you and yours. In the words of an old hymn, *Do not tarry – come to Jesus while you may.*

A prayer then, to end:

Help me to keep those things worth keeping and to be able to recognise them. Forgive me and help me to recover if in the past I have sinned. For your Name's sake.

AMEN

NEVER ALONE

It is a continuing source of amazement to me the number of folk who are awake and listening so early in the morning. Many of you are kind enough to write and tell me how you share your first cup of tea with me each week. One chap, bless him, wrote to say that for him it was Jackson's Tea Deum! Well, first of all thanks for all your scores of letters and bless you for writing. It was, I'm ashamed to say, only recently that another thought really struck me. Not the thought of so many folk being awake, but instead the thought of very many people who never even seem able to go to sleep; and some of them tell me how very much they look forward to the end of the night and hearing 'Prayer for the Day'.

To those of us who normally sleep well and for whom waking up is a far bigger problem than sleeping, it is very difficult to imagine what it's like for those who can't sleep. Speaking personally, I've only known very brief spells of this, and short though they were, my goodness they were bad enough. Some folk can't sleep because of that mysterious problem called insomnia. Some folk can't sleep because of worries, fears, shame – these may be only imaginary but they are very real for those they keep awake through the long night watches. I know from my experience in visiting hospitals that scores upon scores of people do not sleep because of pain of body and some too from the pain of loneliness. A lot of my friends who come to the Mission don't sleep because of the cold, the wet, the noise and being continually moved on. Yes, there's a multitude of folk who look to the morning for relief. It seems better in the daylight, another day may bring what they seek; there's someone to talk to, someone to listen to.

I want to try and say a special word to all such folk and I can best sum it up by assuring you with all the conviction I can command that there is no place where Jesus is NOT, there is no situation that He fails to understand and no person about whom He doesn't care. When you think you are going it all alone, He's there if you want Him, anxious to be your comfort and companion. When you're quite sure there can't possibly be another soul who knows all there is to know about your situation, at that point, because you need Him most, He is nearest at hand.

When you have made your mind up that you must be right outside anybody's love and care, this same Jesus who visited even the damned souls in hell, wants to enfold you with His love, for to Him you are of eternal worth.

So tonight if sleep evades you again, turn your thoughts to Jesus. I and a multitude which no one can number have found Him to be all we need. You see, when we are at the end of our tether God is never at the end of His.

A prayer:

Bless all those, Lord Jesus, who for any reason cannot sleep and dread the long night watches. Make your presence known to them. In the hours of darkness be thou their Light. For your Name's sake.

AMEN

FAILURES LEAGUE

It must mean a great deal to be top of the league – football, cricket, hockey or what have you.

It's because I've always associated the top of the league with winning, with victory, that I got a bit of a shock a few weeks ago. I was reading a local paper up in the north-west and came across an amazing league table. The local authority had drawn up a list of the primary schools under their care and recorded the number of scholars from each of these who had gone on to higher education by passing what is called the eleven plus exam, and at the top of the league was the school who had the least number of successful pupils, the biggest proportion of failures. Now I have really no idea what the local committee deduced from this or why indeed they published such figures, but they certainly set me thinking. Was the best school the one with most scholars to pass the eleven plus?

Is the purpose of a school to enable more children to be so taught as to pass an exam anyway? When they drew up the league were they comparing like with like? How many other factors, if any, ought to be taken into consideration? How important is the eleven plus, or for that matter how important should it be? Well, different folk would give different answers to all these queries; all I want to say as a layman in these things is this. Education as a word truly means to lead out, to draw out; and nowhere in its true sense is there anything remotely meaning to pack, or cram or stuff in.

I'd like to see a league showing the school where children are helped to grow in goodness and kindness. Where boys and girls are helped to appreciate those things which really matter. Where they are led by example to an awareness of what makes for true and lasting happiness.

Where there is enough freedom for the nonconformist to develop his gifts and enough discipline to foster an awareness of the other person. Our world today, our country today,

I know, stands in sore need of citizens growing up who are brilliant and clever, but please God there may be those who are also good and loyal and honest and clean. And if our choice must be one or the other then my vote must go for the latter. Clever devils and brilliant rogues only bring hurt and harm, as is self-evident today. As in so many cases, we are all too ready to ask the wrong questions and to draw up the wrong leagues. Jesus was well educated you know; the Bible says He grew in wisdom and stature. Splendid, but it didn't stop there. It goes on, 'and in favour with God and man'. That's the best education, surely.

A prayer for all who teach and all who learn:

Guide them by the Spirit that both may know and follow Thy way of truth and light, O Lord.

AMEN

FIT FOR HIM?

Those who know me best and love me most always see to it that whatever else I may get or not get at Christmas, I shall at least have one good book, preferably a book of my choice. I must confess that they are not quite unaided in this for well before Christmas I do read aloud the odd book review or ask someone in the right company if they have read such and such lately, and go on to add that I haven't – YET – but that I'd dearly like to.

Up to now its never failed. I mentioned two or three books and ended up with *In and Out of the Box* by Robert Dougall. It came up to my expectations and I've enjoyed reading it very much indeed. There are many, many incidents I would like to comment on but I'm picking one out that for me is memorable.

Robert Dougall tells how on one occasion he was sitting next to a very renowned Church dignitary and was able to ask him some questions. One of the questions which he asked was this: 'Is there one thing in particular that worries you?' It was some little time before he got an answer but when it came it was this. The Archbishop of Canterbury, Dr Michael Ramsey, said, 'Sometimes I lie awake in the middle of the night and I wonder, am I acceptable to God?' When I read that I was in bed; it wasn't the middle of the night but it made me sit up and think and I read it and re-read it.

What would my reply have been to such a question? What would yours have been? The state of the nation is cause enough for worry. So is the future of the world for my grandchildren, the obvious malaise in the Church, the faults and failings of so many folk I know, the seeming hopelessness of much of the work that goes on in my East End Mission in Whitechapel, my personal hopes not fulfilled, the lack of response to what I offer as a Methodist preacher; I could go on and on with my list of worries. If, however, I stop and examine them, by and large they are all about other

3

peoples' failures, the things they have not done or are not doing, the dire and desperate need for alteration on their part. Or else they are worries about me, here and now, in a material and physical world, health, wealth or lack of it to a greater or lesser degree.

What a lesson I learned from Robert Dougall's book. Yet it was something I knew about in the bottom of my heart because when I was a lad of fifteen I heard a great Methodist minister preach. His name was the Rev Alfred Robinson. He ended the sermon by saying that he had only one fear in life and that fear was that at the end of his life when he met God face to face God wouldn't recognise him. When he insisted that he was Alfred Robinson – indeed the Rev Alfred Robinson – his great fear was that God would shake His head and say, 'Ah, but you're not the Alfred Robinson I meant you to be.'

When it comes to what I'm told today is called the 'nitty-gritty', I believe that that's the only worry, the only fear and anxiety worth entertaining in our lives at all.

Am I acceptable to God, am I the me, are you the you, whom God intended us to be?

There's enough there for a Monday morning for any of us to need to pray, so I'll do just that.

Gracious God, who hast made us in thine own image and with a unique place in thine eternal plan, make us daily more fit to be found acceptable in thy sight, through Jesus Christ our Lord.

AMEN

SHE FLOATS

I'm getting a bit tired of all the pressure put upon us in the early part of each year regarding our holidays. The most important issue of the day seems to be 'where are we going this year?' and everywhere promises to be better, bigger, brighter and offers more than anywhere else for a longer time and for less money. To say the least, they can't all be right and I end up quite bewildered and sadly in need of a holiday from the pressures themselves.

I sometimes think a friend of mine had the right answer to holidays. A few years ago it was, he decided to build his own boat, a small cruiser. He laid the keel in his garage one autumn and he laboured long and hard. He told me at the time the number of brass nails he used; it was a staggering figure. As the weeks rolled by I got quite a kick out of watching the boat's progress. I made the extra and unnecessary call sometimes as the months passed just to have a look at the progress. But my word, progress it did and when it came to the varnishing and finishing touches it truly was something to be proud of.

Just a few days before they loaded it on to a trailer which attached to his car, and set off for a quiet spot on the Welsh coast, I recall standing and looking at it and trying – rather feebly I thought at the time – to express my admiration for his patience and workmanship and to congratulate him on the finished article. He himself didn't seem too enthusiastic as I would have been in his place. I would have called all the street in to have a look. I think I understood his calm reticence only when three days after setting off for the coast I got a postcard from him. All it said on it were three words, 'She floats – Hallelujah!' You see, the time to shout about it was not when it looked good, seemed perfect. The time to shout 'Hallelujah' was when, put to the test, it fulfilled what it was designed to do. A good-looking, seemingly perfect craft on dry land is grand to look at. The real test comes when she's in the water and sails the seas as boats should.

One of the reasons why I am telling you this is because I have found something which works. I have put Jesus and His promises to the test and this Christianity works. For me it's more than a theory, it's practical, relevant and even exceeds all expectations. Oh! I have a lot of doubts about me, but never about my Master. I fail regularly, I know, but Jesus never does. I reach the end of my tether, and faith and hope and love seem to recede. But His faith in me, His hope for me, and His love towards me, they are ever faithful, ever sure and like my friend I want to shout 'Hallelujah'. Because this for me is a matter of experience over many years now, I look forward to these opportunities week by week to speak a good word for Jesus. Charles Wesley wrote,

O let me commend my Saviour to you.
I set to my seal that Jesus is true.

– and I say, Hallelujah!
My prayer this morning then:

For a pardon for all my sins, for a peace that passes all understanding, for a power to live now and for evermore, I thank Thee, Lord.

AMEN

UP THE WOLVES

I know that many of you know, so forgive me for telling you again, that I'm a follower of football. When I had more puff than I have now I played regularly, and since then I've watched it here and there and yonder and especially in the halcyon days of Wolves. I have many happy memories of Molineux ground in the grand days of my friend Stan Cullis. Oh! yes, there's a lot, a big lot, about it now that disturbs me greatly; indeed it saddens me because I believe it has made the game the poorer and incidentally lost it a great deal of support. My watching these days is confined to my armchair, a pint mug of tea and the telly. We take it all for granted but for me it's still a miracle to sit at my own fireside and see it all so clear and plain, and I'm most grateful to all who make it possible.

I have the odd smile: it seems they play on the park nowadays not the pitch, and they don't shoot into the corner of the goal they slot the ball into the apex. When somebody actually does this it's better than a variety show to see grown men rush to hug and kiss the scorer. He may well have got £100 and more for doing it but he's treated as though he'd been missing for two years and just made it back from the Arctic wastes. I try to imagine barristers and solicitors doing this when they have just won a case, or shop assistants when they've sold a tea service, or doctors and nurses when they have removed an appendix. However, there it is, but another thing I have noticed is that in nearly every game I manage to see we do appear to have some most excellent goalkeepers, including my namesake. Reporters and commentators tell us of shots well saved. They even go so far as to say the goalkeeper brought off a save that was out of this world. And knowing what they mean I would quite often agree with them.

I'm all for this, because this is what I believe we need a great deal more of – saving by a power that is out of this world.

When there is an election on I listen to all the words, words, words. I remember an election years ago when I asked my Dad what difference it would make and he replied, 'One lot of sinners in and another lot of sinners out.' He didn't mean that MPs are worse sinners than everyone else, what he did mean was that we all need a Saviour. This does include MPs and if ever there was a time when we needed men of God, good men to lead our nation, surely it is now. If ever we had proved up to the hilt how inevitable is the mess and morass a nation can get into that more and more leaves out God, surely it is now. One of the truths revealed in history and perhaps more especially in recent history is that this is God's world, this is God's nation and it will only walk properly God's way. We need to be saved; we need to be saved by someone out of this world if victory is to come to us in the end. So I end by praying for all our Members of Parliament.

Gracious God, who has made us and who does love us all, look graciously upon our Parliament. By thy living Spirit move and guide their hearts and minds according to thy Holy and loving will, that upheld and directed by thee they may do that and only that which is well pleasing in thy sight. Through Jesus Christ our Lord.

AMEN

PITY MY SIMPLICITY

At several big stations where I worked when I was a railway-man there was a man employed who was called the rat-catcher. They called him that for the perfectly good reason that it was his job to catch rats. Incidentally it was a special-ised and very much needed work that he did – well, he and his ferrets. Then there came a historic day, a cataclysmic event I think you might have called it. They changed his title to rodent operative. I'm not clear even after all these years why, because you see, his job was still to catch rats!

Some time ago now I came across a verse that was new to me at any rate.

> *Coruscate, scintillate, globule vivific.*
> *Fain would I fathom your nature specific;*
> *Loftily poised in the ether capacious,*
> *Strongly resembling a gem carbonaceous.*

I hadn't a clue what it was all about until my friend who gave it to me said it was something I used to say in Sunday School – a modern version of it, as it were. I wasn't any better off so then he broke into song,

> *Twinkle, twinkle little star,*
> *How I wonder what you are*
> *Up above the world so high*
> *Like a diamond in the sky.*

Who would have thought you could have made that simple verse of a hymn into anything so complicated?

My Dad used to tell me about a goods guard on the rail-way who was often in trouble with his superiors. You see, it is the duty of any goods guard if his train has a derailment to send in a written report of what happened to his superiors. This particular guard, Mr Flanigan by name, was often in trouble because always his reports were long, wordy and

39

tedious. For some time they pleaded with him to no avail, but in the end he got the message. After a derailment he sent a letter to head office that read, 'Off again, on again, away again, Flanigan.' No man could have covered it more succinctly than that, could they?

I believe my job is to speak a good word for Jesus, indeed that's what I try to do each Monday morning as the great privilege comes along. I made my mind up years ago now that the devil wasn't going to have a monopoly of the use of four letter words, that there is a true and eternal simplicity in the gospel, the good news which I preach. Here are some simple truths: 'God is love', 'I am His and He is mine for ever', 'He loved me and gave Himself for me'. Jesus said, 'I am the Way, the Truth and the Life.' Was there any wonder the common people heard him gladly, that fishermen forsook all and followed Him, that a harlot knew what He was talking about? Is there any wonder that for almost twenty centuries common folk have gone on understanding Him and lived and laboured – aye, and often have died for Him? Is there any wonder that after all those years I'm talking now about Him? Is there any wonder too that so many have *not* followed Him when the Church has buried Him in increasing polysyllabic profundity? Is there any wonder that more and more common men have turned their backs on Him and said, 'I go a fishing'?

I know the Old Testament is about ethical monotheism but I'd rather tell you it's a book about one good God. I know the New Testament tells of an Incarnation but I'd rather tell you that Jesus was a chip off the old block. Please hear about Him simply and gladly today and then ask Him,

> *Pity my simplicity.*
> *Suffer me to come to thee.*

AMEN

TIGHTEN YOUR BELTS

Whatever the future may bring either of marvel or surprise, at least we can all be assured of the need to make do with less. We have been told time and time again that we're sailing into rough seas, and struggle and sacrifice will be called for from all good men and true. Personally I don't think that will do the majority much harm; I can but hope it will apply equally to every man. Yet on that I must confess, I wonder! 'Tighten your belts' is the clarion cry and all talk of surplus, extra, more and bigger and better, these are things of the past for the time being at any rate. One man I was listening to recently on this subject, put it this way. He said, 'For as far ahead as I can see the time for all extravagances has gone.'

I think I know what he was trying to tell us and in the sense in which he meant it, it could be very, very true. I want to go on to say that if ever there was a time when extravagances were needed I believe that time is right now.

Off and on during these recent years I have watched and am still watching my children as they try to teach their children that something which is usually referred to as manners. They tell them there are two magic words called 'please' and 'thank you' and they encourage them to use them in the right places. So they should, but really you know it's not only children who need to be so taught. I'm coming across more and more adults who are almost devoid of any manners at all. I believe this world is a better place when folk are better mannered and I'm positive there is no such person as a bad-mannered Christian – so let's have an extravagance in manners.

I would also like to plead for an extravagance in doing something for nothing. First of all doing something for the sheer joy of doing it, not just do-it-yourself because it's cheaper, but doing something – it might only be watching a sunset and studying a rosebud or watching the laughter and play of little children – just for its own sake. Or else doing something, not for yourself, not for gain or profit, but free for somebody else. Service, which means to a greater or lesser degree, sacrifice on your part. Something like, not just putting the old folk down the road in touch with meals-on-wheels, good though that certainly is, but taking them or inviting them to a bit of your meal, not just arranging a home-help for them but you going and you helping them in their home on the odd occasion. Not sitting in with the very young and the very old at so much an hour but doing it for free for those who can't even pay so much an hour. You know, I can remember when life was much more like that and it was so because in the hearts and lives of many folk there was an extravagance of selfless service.

We tend to overlook the courtesy of Jesus, the respect He had for other people and the lesson He taught on good manners. We tend to overlook those words in the New Testament which say very simply that He went about doing good. Not always preaching, not always praying, not always at worship in the house of God, not always reciting the Commandments, but always extravagant in gentlemanliness, always extravagant in watching the lilies and the wheat and the mustard tree and the birds, always extravagant in stretching out a hand to those who were in any kind of need.

Well, it seems we shall feel the pinch, but don't let us pinch in manners and service.

A prayer then to end:

Bless us, Lord Jesus, as we try to be good in our manners and in our service for your name's sake.

AMEN

SARAH'S BIRTHDAY

The day that is for me first and foremost my granddaughter Sarah's birthday is for very many folk bonfire night, Guy Fawkes Day, the day of Gunpowder Plot and all that. I do want to say 'Take care,' because so many always get hurt this day and then go on to say, fancy keeping it up all these years, celebrating as it were the foiled attempts of a man to destroy Parliament, law and order. Oh yes! Maybe in those days he was justified, and I know that there are good laws and bad laws and I know too that sincere men have fought and died to change unjust laws, and thank God for them. Nevertheless, I'm sure that many good folk are extremely bothered because so very many people believe that all you need to do today is to please yourself, to do your own thing, to do just as *you* please, and to express yourself as you will.

Well let me assure you that among the reasons for my being a Protestant and a nonconformist is the deep love and fervour I have in my heart for freedom.

If we go back to Sarah's birthday, on that day she's free to open her birthday cards and presents I'm sure, but not to do it with Dad's razor blade. She's free to blow out the candles on her cake, but not to set light to the dining room curtains with them. Free to have a party tea, but not to eat it all herself.

I once heard about a chap who was taking his car for the first time on a continental holiday and heard they drove 'over there' on the right side of the road. He then changed his mind, much to the surprise of his mates at work, and when they asked why, he said he'd been for a trial run down the right hand side of a motorway near his home and very nearly got killed. Just so, there are vital basic freedoms we must ever preserve and indeed men have died for them and would again, but there does come a point when freedom ceases to be such and becomes licence. It can be not only harmful but even fatal.

There has never been a greater protagonist for freedom

than Jesus. Indeed they crucified Him mainly for this very thing. He broke the shackles of a rigorous, cold, meaningless legalistic system. He boiled down the contemporary system of hundreds of laws into two commandments. It is within these two commandments and only within them that I covet freedom for myself and for all men. Let any man anywhere keep those rules of loving God utterly, and therefore his fellow man, and then he's truly free to do just what he likes. He's not only happy in his freedom, he is also bringing nothing but happiness to other people. Somebody put it very simply by saying, 'Love God and do as you like.' Another said, 'Jesus, whose service is perfect freedom.'

To go back again to Sarah's birthday, I'm pretty sure she and her brother will have some fireworks. Well, even I can still remember that there are two kinds of fireworks – the bangers and the beauties. Sarah will be having only the beauties. You see the bangers can hurt and scar and blind, the others can bring colour and light and loveliness.

The freedom which is licence may well go off with a bang and cause a stir but so often it wounds and scars. The other kind of freedom which is there in all its fullness within the love of Jesus is something of beauty and colour, of fulfilment and satisfaction. Accept the kingly rule of the love of Jesus and then and only then please yourself.

A prayer to end:

Rule in all our hearts and lives, Lord Jesus, and grant us the freedom that is only perfected in your service.

AMEN

THE CREED

I did something a week or so ago that gave me a great deal of pleasure. I sent in an order to a bookseller for sixty new books. One of my great loves is books and I can't begin to tell you the joy that has come to me through reading. My wife says sometimes in her weaker moments that I've got more than enough books and has even gone so far as to hint that if I get more and more of them she would consider leaving me! But as I keep telling her, I'm the best husband she's ever had. But don't get alarmed. She's not going to be confronted with another sixty books, because the order which I despatched was for Methodist hymn books for my church. The pleasure over the transaction was because many of those we have got are badly worn, which means they have been well used and also sometimes we have just not got enough and that in itself is another very good thing.

But when you come to order new hymn books there are decisions to make. What colour do you want them to be? What size do you prefer, what style of paper and print? Well, I made these decisions and then I found you could have them lettered in gold, and additional lettering could be embossed on them which gives the name of your church or the words 'For the use of visitors'. Well, it's all cleared up now and I look forward to our having and using these new books.

While I was engaged in this transaction I was reminded of something that I came across in Cornwall a few years ago when I was on holiday down there.

On the inside of the cover of the hymn book which I was given as I entered the church, there was THE CREED, the things which I believe about God and His Church and indeed about me and about you. But that wasn't all; this church had purchased a rubber stamp made up of rather bold capitals and they had used it on front and back inside covers. So diagonally across the Creed which, as I said is a recital of all I believe, I read the words NOT TO BE TAKEN

AWAY. What a blasphemy it is when things do turn out like that, isn't it? When in church I say 'I believe in God the Father Almighty' and so on, and then I go on my way and DON'T take it away. I go on my way and I do ungodly things, I forget that He is my Father and every man's Father, and that therefore every man is my brother, be he next door or starving in Ethiopia or wounded and dying in Northern Ireland or the Middle East.

I tell God I believe He's Almighty and then don't take that great truth away and I let doubts and fears creep into my soul and I live as though evil will always win and as though love, truth and justice must fail, I mourn as one without hope, and fear death in spite of saying in my creed that I believe in Jesus who rose again from the dead and promised and prepared for me a life everlasting with Him.

The Creed is to be taken away – it has to do with Monday as well as Sunday. It has to do with washing days, working days, as well as worship days. It belongs in my house and yours during the week as well as in God's House on Sunday morning.

Please, please don't read the Creed if you don't intend to heed it.

Our prayer today:

God the Father Almighty, make our creed and deed one, every day.

AMEN

46

ACROSS CLAPS

Someone I knew in my boyhood, now living in Wales, wrote to me recently and also sent me a postcard on which was a picture of the chapel where I grew up in more ways than one, and where too I was married. It had been sent to her years and years ago and on the back it said, 'love from Nellie and Jessie'. Now Nellie and Jessie were sisters and my cousins. Funny how a little thing like that starts you thinking. I went back to my boyhood days and all sorts of memories came flooding back and among those memories I recalled the scores of times when as a lad I had gone across the 'claps'.

Let me explain. Very near to where I lived and next door but one to the home of my cousins there was a pathway, a public footpath. After you had walked a good half mile between fields you came to the railway, the main line from Crewe to Carlisle. To cross the line you had to pass on either side of the railway through a gate and these were gates with clap-hatches, so this particular walk through those gates was always spoken of locally as going across claps. We readily and often dispensed with definite articles in my neck of the woods.

I began to think about those days and that walk especially during the long summer holidays. You watched Fitton's cattle – Fitton was a local butcher and farmer – maybe you ate some of them the Sunday following, I often wondered. But when you had gone through the clap-hatches then if you continued over stiles and through gates it was perhaps two miles before you came to the road again. All the way it was grass and shrubs and spinneys and corn and the like. I've lain on my back there on a baking hot day and watched and listened to a skylark as it soared and sang, a bit of a contrast to Whitechapel Road I'll assure you. I found birds' nests and marvelled at the skill that went into building them and secluding them. I've wandered off the narrow path and found – and my goodness how difficult a job it is – a plover's nest on a dusty ploughed field and seen the craftiness of the plover returning to her eggs but alighting far away and zig-zagging to it, camouflaged by her own colouring against the soil. I've seen rabbits play and pheasants strut and partridges scurry, and almost every recollection of going across claps is a memory of loveliness and peace.

Yet there were odd times, I'm not sure quite why, when we didn't go across directly and out at Bostock. Instead, we'd trespass to go and see the pit. Well away from the public footpath and well hidden was a pit, or tip, into which was thrown offal, animal skins, rubbish, and it was foul and smelly and rotten and especially so on a hot summer day.

As I say, I'm not sure, as I look back, why we digressed into such foulness. I only know we did, we sought out pollution.

To a greater and lesser degree we all do this. There's beauty and loveliness to behold and we turn aside to the sordid and cheap. Oh! I know that sometimes, maybe more often than not, it's only in our minds; but we do it none the less. There are good and grand things to see in someone's character, and we root about to find something rotten. There's music in life, and laughter like the singing of a lark on a summer day, and we're listening to germ-bearing flies buzzing round rotteness.

There are things which pollute our minds and bodies and we're found there when we could be amongst the columbine, the honeysuckle and the hawthorn and buttercups and daisies, the beautiful things in life and in our fellows.

Jesus said there's a way to Hell and a way to Heaven and He says He's the latter way.

So let's end by asking Him,

Show us Thy way, O Lord, and help us to walk in it.

AMEN

BUILDING SOCIETY

My Dad had a queer way of remembering when he had to pay it. I'm pretty sure, though, that it was most effective and I don't think that a month ever passed without my parents honouring their obligation. But it was queer to me as a lad to hear them say they always paid on the first Friday after the second Monday. Yet as I say, it never failed and that was the evening when one of them went along and paid their dues at the Building Society. In those days of course you could buy a nice house, bathroom, bay window and three bedroomed semi, for a bit over £500. And I suppose their monthly dues were in what is now the 50p to 60p bracket. I wonder are we any better off? I very very much wonder.

Well, goodness knows we hear a great deal about Building Societies. Mortgage rates, interest rates, staggered interest repayments, only money out if money in, whatever all that and the rest means. What it does mean for sure is that far, far too many young couples wishing, and rightly so, to set up in a home of their own are finding it virtually impossible to do so. I don't think the problem is just an economic one any longer, it has become a very serious moral issue and I for one wish I could see it being tackled as such for the good of our land and its future, for I believe the only true foundation on which you can build a good country is upon hearthstones.

But that is not all I want to say about Building Societies; I am concerned about a moral problem that can only be solved by building society – and not in the bricks, mortar, mortgage sense. Instead, in the sense of building society up in the Christian faith, in the way of Jesus.

All too many people are contributing to and talking about a promiscuous society, a decadent society, an affluent society, a technological society. Let's be hearing far more about building society.

There was a time when men had as their belief (more

often than not because many of them were Christians) a belief which said in effect, 'I've got a meat and potato pie, is there anybody about who has only got a knife and fork and no pie?' I don't find it to be like that so much now. Now all too many folk are saying 'I've got a knife and fork, who's got all the meat and potato pies?'

I want to help in Building Society by levelling up, not levelling down. A society where greed and grab and grasp give way to caring and sharing, where having and holding and hogging give place to helping and healing and heeding. A society where the 'have-nots' are not driven to despair, because the 'haves' are compassionate, where the 'haves' are not just intent on having more but are intent on helping more.

I want to help in Building Society that knows man does not live by bread alone, that things do rust and decay and are stolen, and that real treasure is never man-given but God-given in Jesus Christ.

My work in East London isn't just on the first Friday after the second Monday, it's all the time because through Christ we are engaged in Building Society, and here's a prayer to end.

Lord Jesus Christ, help us to invest our lives in your love and take interest only in sharing that love. Borrow us, all we have and are, and make us profitable servants.

AMEN

DO-IT-YOURSELF

Because I'm a minister and because I think I know what that word 'minister' means, because I live and work where I do, because I know there are lots and lots of people including the very old and the very young who are quite beyond being able to do anything for themselves; because I know all this I dare to go on to say that there are times when I want to remind some folk that this is a 'Do-it-yourself' age. I want to remind some of them that if they are really serious when they say they want a helping hand then I can tell them where to find one, indeed better still, I can tell them where to find two; they are both within easy reach, they are in fact at the ends of their arms.

I'm meeting an increasing number of folk upon whom it seems this simple, honest, plain fact has not, as yet, dawned. Far too often the cry goes up, 'THEY ought to do this or that', THEY always being someone other than themselves.

I'm old enough to remember what is sometimes referred to as the Hungry Thirties, and I can recall that most damnable blot on our history books called the 'Means Test'. If that title means that it was the meanest thing man ever did to his fellow man, then it was quite right so to name it. Yet having said all that, I have got to go on to say something else. Where I live you frequently hear all the dirty four letter words there are and I've come to the conclusion that there's hardly anything left either to see or to hear that would shock me any more. I do however both deplore and regret an increasing attitude that seems to be very prevalent, of regarding the word 'WORK' as a dirty word these days. There are those who seem to act as if it were another form of plague to be shunned and from which one should keep as far away as possible.

I've always been delighted whenever I have reflected on Jesus and His earliest followers that they were a sort of working mens' club, a carpenter, fishermen, tax-gatherer, healer and later joined by a tent-maker. For this fact neither

Jesus nor any of His followers ever made any excuse. To them what they did was honourable. The tent-maker went so far as to say that the true followers of Jesus must be 'workmen who need not be ashamed'. If a man can't work and would if he could, that is a moral issue and should be tackled as such with whoever is responsible. If a man could work but won't then that is the man to whom we have a duty to say, 'Do it yourself'.

If I had a song about a few of my favourite things, or memories, they would not first of all be flying over the Alps, walking up Pennsylvania Avenue, or even standing on the Mount of Olives. No, I like to recall a farmer ploughing a field or rearing pigs, well. A potter making a vase, well. A collier, hewing at the coal face, well. A cotton spinner or a lace maker, doing it well. An honest garage man doing a good service. A teacher preparing for tomorrow's class, well. A man putting shelves up, decorating a room, a mother bathing a baby or knitting it a poncho, well. The man brushing the road, mending shoes, well. The doctors in the great London Hospital where I am privileged to be chaplain, the nurses and all the folk who work there, making folk WELL.

You, whatever you must do today and what for you is work, will you be doing it well?

Remember this,

> The daily round, the common task
> Will furnish all you need to ask –
> Room to deny yourself; a road
> That brings you daily nearer God.

A prayer:

Help us to remember that the good workers of the world do unite with God.

AMEN

DR JOAN

It was the day before she was to undergo a major heart operation that I saw her first. The lady herself was a doctor, what's more she was a Christian doctor who for many years had worked overseas as a medical missionary. For a while we just chatted and most interesting it was too, for would you believe it, her father had been the minister of Queen Street Church in Wolverhampton where I had been minister of Darlington Street. Then, she said, he left there and went as minister to St George's Church in Bolton and after I left those happy years in Wolverhampton I too went to Bolton to the Victoria Hall. It stopped there. The doctor's father next went to Cardiff, I think she said, and I went to the Albert Hall, Nottingham.

Well the next day she had her operation. I was going to say, 'alas she died.' But I can't say 'alas', for she spoke with such confidence and joy about life after death that it would be a mockery to both her faith and her memory if I said 'alas' as if her passing were all loss. She had reminded me in her conversation that she knew just about as many people in heaven as she did on earth and death held no terrors for her. On the contrary, while not wishing to die just now, if it so happened then still for her all was well.

Do you know, I've met lots of people like that and their kind of faith and trust and hope is something we are in danger of losing. They said of those early Methodists that they died well, and Charles Wesley wrote a hymn the first line of which sums it all up: 'Rejoice for a brother deceased, our loss is his infinite gain.' A faith and hope like that surely sparkles and is radiant. All this that I'm saying to you was prompted not only by meeting the doctor I've just told you about but also by a word or two in a recent letter which was sent to me. The kindly writer mentioned how glad she was that I was well and at work and on the air again and then wrote, 'while I do not begrudge you one moment of heaven, may you long continue.' Fancy that, she didn't want me to lose any of the promised bliss of heaven. How many of us do really feel, because of Jesus, like that about heaven? The Bible is almost reticent in what it tells us about heaven but for me it says more than enough. In a word or two it states very simply that Jesus will be there and that all who go there will both know and be known in His presence and as new people in their Father's House. Well now, that will do for me when the time comes, so as I think of my loved ones who have died, I *do* know where but don't know when, 'but I know we'll meet again some happy day.'

When Columbus was sailing west into the unknown his sailors grew tired and homesick and afraid and they say he kept urging them on as he pointed to the west by saying over and over again, 'There's life beyond the sunset, there's life beyond the sunset,' and one day, you remember, they did arrive.

I believe that more and more every day, and if you ask me how I know it's true, I'm not evading the issue when I say 'I know that I know' and such blessed assurance is more than enough for me.

A prayer then to end.

Lord Jesus Christ, who art alive for evermore and who hast said, 'Because I live you too shall live,' strengthen our faith and increase our hope until that day when we are reunited with those whom we have loved and lost awhile and share with them the glory and the wonder which they already know of beholding thee face to face.

AMEN

BY-PRODUCTS

I suppose it has been the so-called fuel crisis which has reminded me of my boyhood days. Days during which you could go to the gas works with sixpence (old money I mean, of course) and a wheel-barrow and come back without the sixpence but with the wheel-barrow filled with coke.

You could also go to the gas works with a bucket and it wasn't in order to get a bucket full of gas either, it was to get a bucket of gas tar with which to tar the roof of the shed.

Gas works – a funny place to go for coke and tar? I used to think that because I had not heard then of things called by-products. Those things produced at the gas works, gas, coke, tar, are all by-products of coal. I believe there are other by-products of coal in addition to those. Indeed, I am given to understand that in the realm of industry there are some really fascinating and amazing by-products being produced. We can see and shall see even more into the realm of by-products of oil, for it seems that when the price of oil is put up, the prices of many by-products must inevitably rise to.

Perhaps you have never heard the story of the family, dad, mother and little girl, who decided one year to have a camping holiday in Scotland. They found a lovely spot and pitched their tent nearby a mountain stream. Day by day Dad went to the stream with his water can to collect the fresh clear water they needed and each time the little girl went to the stream with him. All she had got to fetch the water in was a child's wicker shopping basket and when Dad dipped in the can and filled it she dipped in the basket and needless to say all the water ran away straight through the mesh. Dad and Mum used to smile quietly each time she went with Dad, and after a day or two they said, 'You don't bring much water back in your basket do you?' The little lass paused for a while and then she said, 'No I don't do I; but look, my basket has got a lot cleaner hasn't it?'

and so it had. I reckon you could call that a by-product, couldn't you?

This is why I make a plea for our reading good books rather than a lot of filth. This is why I believe that listening to conversation that is wholesome and decent is much better than wallowing in conversational muck. I'm more than sure that the kind of company we keep, the sort of friendships we make, do matter a great deal. The by-products of our reading, our speaking, our friendships are to be seen eventually in our own lives, in our own characters. I think the by-products of public worship in church are of great value in addition to the direct influences for good that going to God's house has upon us. The by-products of some occupations are truly dreadful, such as pneumoconiosis for the miners and once upon a time, silicosis for the pottery workers.

The by-products of all evil are even more fatal and widespread.

The by-products of the good way, of God's way, are peace and joy and fulfilment and purpose and satisfaction. Being a Christian is not and should never be an insurance policy for either here or hereafter; but who am I to grumble if I discover as I have that in following Jesus there are many, many by-products? Call them bonuses if you like.

A prayer to end, then.

Whatsoever things are lovely, pure, just, honest and of good report, help us to think on these things, Lord Jesus, for this is your way. And for all the good things to come to us in so doing, accept our grateful thanks.

AMEN

STATION MASTER

Over recent weeks I've had more time than I've ever had, I think, to do what I once heard of a certain man doing as his normal way of life.

When asked what he did he replied, 'One of two things: sometimes I sits and thinks and at other times I just sits.' Well, as I say I've done a lot of that and one day when just sitting and thinking for no reason that I remember, I began to think about Crewe Station of all places. I worked there for a time as my father had done years and years before. I helped to wire up the loudspeakers on the public address system and I remember the Irish Mail leaving the rails one day and very nearly ending up in the refreshment rooms – tea twopence a cup then!

In those days the station master was Major Cowley. I can see him now in tail-coat and striped trousers, wearing a tall hat and carrying his gloves and always wearing a button-hole. Smart, immaculate, a man with a presence but he was also a man proud of the company he worked for and as its representative he brought to it nothing but credit. His dress was his uniform just as much as that of the porter or guard; every day he sought to be a credit to it, and as far as I know, every day he was. He knew the people saw him and he was seen at his best.

But one day on platform five a shackler, the man who couples up and uncouples carriages, was crushed between the buffers when doing his job. Major Cowley happened to be near by and without a moment's hesitation he jumped down from the platform on the line and went to the aid of his fellow workman. In no time at all there was dirt and oil and blood on his normally spotless clothes and he cradled the man's head until further help came.

Perhaps I remembered him because it was coming up towards Easter. I suppose in a sense God up there, sitting on a throne, high and lifted up, is a wonderful thought. But what about when we get damaged and crushed and broken?

Where is He then, all dressed up as it were above the bright blue sky? Oh no! for Easter has reminded me again that He – God – has suffered. He too has been down here in the dirt and muck and injuries of life. He's been stained with blood and mixed up to the hilt in this thing called Life; aye and in this thing we call Death too.

If you read the *Journal*, the diary of John Wesley's life, the most oft repeated entry is, 'I offered them Christ'. You know, that's really the sum total of the job of being a minister. For me that is the sole purpose of this book, that I might offer to all of you Jesus Christ. Not immaculate and aloof, but one who has been where and what we are, so that you and I could become what He is.

Let's talk to Him a moment.

Lord Jesus, we are glad to know that nothing happening to us is outside your understanding. Come into our hearts and lives now as Saviour and Lord.

AMEN

58

REAL BOWLS

Even though I've often been told it's an old man's game I've never accepted it, for I played first in my very early teens. We had a team belonging to the chapel to which I belonged. I'm talking about bowls. I've not played much since I became a Methodist minister and left home, the main reason being that ever since I did leave home, wherever I've lived subsequently they have played another kind of bowls.

In Cheshire, where I began bowling, you play on a crown green and bowl the jack; the others play on a flat green and place the jack. I think crown green is far more difficult, the force of gravity has also to be contended with. However, in both cases the key factor is something called BIAS. Your bowls, or woods, are biassed so that if you bowl them straight they are so weighted on one side that they will always pull that way. You can have bowls with stronger or weaker bias and the serious player has and knows his own bowls and what they will do. I have still got my father's bowls and I know 'em.

I think this has all come back to me more and more of late because time and time again I find folk saying to me, 'Oh! you are biassed, you're a parson;' or 'You're a Christian.' And you know, I always make the same reply, 'Yes, of course I'm biassed. I'm biassed towards Jesus, towards His love and His teaching.'

I'm biassed as I look at the contemporary scene in our world, to say there is basically only one thing wrong with it and that thing is what Jesus called SIN.

I'm biassed enough to believe too with all my heart that there is only one answer to all the problems in our world and that answer is a person – Jesus Christ the one and only Saviour of the world.

I hear a great deal today about people being allowed to 'do their thing', and believe it or not I'm biassed enough to believe that the Church's thing today, and indeed my thing, is to offer Christ, or as Charles Wesley puts it in one of his grand hymns, 'O let me commend my Saviour to you.' This is what I call my Master's business and therefore it is my business in word and deed and I'm biassed enough to believe that anything less than that is fake and gimmick and must inevitably fail.

But above all I'm biassed enough to believe and to know, because I have proved it, that if I do accept him as my Lord and Saviour He will honour His promises and nothing else really matters at all.

Well, I shall watch them bowling again here and there during the summer and I shall say, 'Thank God I'm biassed too.'

A prayer now.

Draw us to yourself, Lord Jesus, and then, having accepted you as Saviour and Lord, hold us and keep us in your way, and keep us ever biassed on the Godward side.

AMEN

THANK GOD

Monday, I know, is still traditionally washing day in many parts of the country and if it is in yours I hope you have what my mother used to call 'a good drying day', especially for the whites.

The weather is perhaps all too often a subject for conversation in this country. We tend to moan a great deal about it and yet, you know, we really are most fortunate for it's very, very rarely that we get any severe and dangerous extremes. All of which leads me on to a story I came across some time ago.

It seems that in this Methodist circuit from which my story comes, they had a renowned local preacher. There are two sorts of preachers in Methodism, ministers and local preachers; somebody once said that ministers were paid to be good and local preachers were good for nothing! Joking apart, they are a wonderful band who take seven out of every ten of our Sunday services – God bless 'em. But I'm wandering. This local preacher in my story was renowned for the fact that he was always bubbling over with gratitude and thankfulness, always praising the Lord for His goodness and loving kindness.

Well, one February Sunday night it was a real brute, sleet and wind and ice here and there and a lazy wind that went through you rather than round. When he went up the pulpit steps the congregation numbered TWO and one of them leaned over to the other and said, 'He'll have nowt to thank God for tonight.' They sang the first hymn and then came the prayer. The preacher began, 'We thank Thee, O Loving Heavenly Father, that it is very rarely that the weather is as bad as it is tonight.'

So you see, he did find something to be thankful for. I know I do my share of moaning. It would be easy to dwell on life's frets and worries. Maybe wet washing days do seem to come round more frequently than dry ones. Yet, I make a plea for a much deeper sense of gratitude not only to God but to our fellows, and maybe especially within the home and family circle. Do you say 'Thank you' for a good Sunday dinner and a clean shirt to put on?

Of this I am quite sure for I've proved it so very often, that throughout any day there will be lots and lots of times when we shall need to be thankful. If you choose you can stub your toe on the bed-post when you get up and let that blacken all the day; or you can look through the window and jump for joy. A new day in which to love and care and share and help, another day in which you are sure to prove the promises of Jesus are faithful and true.

Indeed, if you're listening to me, be grateful for that. All the deaf folk who can't would be thankful to have your ability to hear.

God can hear, so only a short prayer to him today.

Thank you God for everything.

AMEN

JEWELS RESET

Over the years I have had to drive up and down the country and more often than not it has been on my own. I find this very boring and I try all sorts of ways to relieve this without at the same time diverting my attention from my driving. I've re-lived some of what Sir Neville Cardus calls 'days in the sun' at Old Trafford. I've recalled to mind the saints I have known up and down Methodism. I've found renewed joy in some of the wonderful actions and sayings of my grandchildren.

But I've also passed hour after hour over the years singing. Those who know me best and indeed love me most think this is great for they tell me most forcibly that when I'm alone in a motor car is the ONLY place where I ought to sing! Be that as it may, among my repertoire are some of the hymns we used to sing when I was a Sunday school scholar. Recently I had one such hymn stick in my mind and fairly often of late I've sung it over. I wonder if many of you recall it: 'When He cometh, when He cometh to make up His jewels, All His jewels, precious jewels, His loved and His own . . . ' and so on!

Working where I do in Whitechapel, I come into contact every day with many who might be labelled 'unredeemed humanity'. We touch bottom as it were in our catchment area. Sometimes when I find myself asking, 'Is it worthwhile? What am I doing here? Why go on wasting my time? Why not go to the seaside?' I find then it helps me to remember that all these folk are potential jewels in the sight of Jesus. He regards them as gems to be saved and polished. He has given to them all priceless and eternal worth. Just as you have to dig for diamonds, so you have to dig long and hard to find any lustre among these folk. Yet underneath, says Jesus, they are made in the image of His Father, God. I like that bit in the hymn, 'His loved and His own'. Because, you see, so many of my friends down the East End believe that they are not loved and they are not His own, indeed they believe they are not anybody's and nobody cares.

It could easily be that you also feel that you are going it alone, that nobody gives a tuppenny cuss about you. You may be quite sure in your own mind that nowhere is there someone who loves you, no one who calls you His own.

Let me try to persuade you in these few moments we have together that you are quite wrong. Jesus knows *you*, loves *you* and *you* are one of His own.

I'll end with a prayer for my Whitechapel friends and for you.

Lord Jesus, I'm asking you now to speak personally to all those who think nobody loves them and that they are quite alone. Assure them of a place in your love and in your great family. Use me and many others to bring them home. Reset and polish them, your jewels. For your Name's sake.

AMEN

PIG EXPERT

I wonder how many of you get confused in these modern days, these times which are often referred to as a technological age. Folk talk to me about gross and net and per cent, Value Added Tax, surcharges, capital gains, and all I can do quite often is to try and look intelligent and hope to nod in the right places. What I'm saying is, it's easy to get lost outside your own sphere.

In spite of the fact that I was trained at the finest theological college in the Methodist Church, more and more nowadays I find myself outside my sphere, having to deal with things that were never even thought of or mentioned in my training.

I need now to know quite a bit about court procedure, social workers' responsibilities, alcoholism. I write more letters to the Home Office than I do to the British and Foreign Bible Society or the Methodist Missionary Society. I find it all very fascinating yet sometimes it is also very perplexing.

Think about this: who would ever have thought when I was doing my studies of ethics, Old and New Testament, Greek and the like that one day my phone, the phone of a Methodist superintendent minister, would ring and a voice – indeed the voice of one of my staff – would say, 'I think we must sell some of our pigs'? No, he wasn't being rude about anybody connected with the Church, he really was talking about pigs – large white and large white crossed with land-race to be precise – and he was asking my opinion about our selling some. Now here was a sphere they never even touched upon at Richmond College so what could I do, bluff and say, 'Yes, I think it's a good week for selling', or, 'No, let the market improve'? Well, since I wasn't sure I said, 'I'll ring you back, leave it to me.' Then I rang up my good friend Alex in the midlands, and to talk pigs to him is like talking football to Sir Alf Ramsey. I don't suppose any man anywhere knows more about pigs; he will both forgive me and understand if I tell you that he has lived with them all his life. Well, he did help me, and he will go on doing so as I try to do the right thing about pigs. In a word, what I did was the only wise thing to do, I called in the expert.

Now I have found that life is very complicated and confusing today in the sheer business of living. Important decisions are called for, deep understanding is required from time to time and I find I can only go on if I call in the expert. My grandfather would have said, 'Guide me O thou great Jehovah;' my grandson says 'Gentle Jesus meek and mild, look upon a little child.' I say, 'Show me thy way, O Lord, and make it plain.' I've been doing that now for half a century and He's never let me down and always, yes always, when I've taken His advice and followed His guidance everything has worked out all right.

Living for me, and maybe for you, is a sphere in which I cannot go it alone and I must and I can and I do call in the expert. Let's do so now.

Lead us, Lord Jesus, so that we may not only travel aright but also arrive this day and always.

AMEN

CORONATION ROW

I remember, I remember the house where I was born. It was in Coronation Row. There is too a little window at the side, but I don't think it was there when we lived there, so I can't tell you if the sun came peeping in at morn. I do remember too that if on Saturday afternoons at certain times of the year you went upstairs into the front bedroom you could see about one third or maybe half of Winsford United football ground. I've watched parts of many a Cheshire League football match from that bedroom window.

It was a thrill to see a goal scored, providing of course that it was a Winsford player who scored it. I could see them scored at one end and I had to rely on the shouting to tell me when we had scored at the other end. Yet, here's a strange thing, there was for me a bigger thrill than a goal being scored.

Between our house and the football ground there was the recreation ground where I myself first played football and sometimes someone on the proper ground would kick the ball over the stand (the standing up covered stand that is) and on to the 'Rec', as we called our recreation ground. I used to hope and pray that one day I'd play on the big ground and kick the ball over the stand. What a silly ambition as I think about it now. Well, believe it or not the day did come when I did play on that ground; only a friendly match, mind you, but play I did and what's more I realised my ambition.

My little grandson's current ambition followed our buying him a policeman's helmet. I taught him a little ditty my Dad taught me:

> *I wish I were a Bobby*
> *Dressed in Bobby' clothes,*
> *With a big tall hat and a belly full o' fat*
> *And an india-rubber nose.*

Another man who wanted to get away from it all and to contract out as it were, wrote,

> *I wish I were a pedlar man*
> *With a horse to drive and a caravan.*

St Paul had several ambitions. 'I must see Rome,' he wrote on one occasion.

I've fulfilled one or two ambitions. I wanted to ride on the footplate of the Royal Scot Engine, No. 6100, and I did. I wanted to go to the Holy Land and I've been.

I wanted to be a Methodist preacher, I ask no higher state than this, and I am. I wanted to do what John Wesley did and to offer men Christ, and I do.

But above everything I want one day to hear my Saviour say to me, 'Well done.' That's my greatest and my unfulfilled ambition yet.

Now how about you? I'm sure that you have maybe several good or even silly ambitions, like mine to boot a football over and out of a football ground. I want to plead with you to have a big ambition, something not only for time but for eternity, not only for here but also for yonder, something imperishable and indestructible. I want you to want to be today and henceforth Christ's man, Christ's woman. The entrance fee is nothing but the annual subscription is everything.

Let's ask Him to help us so to do.

Come into our hearts and lives, Lord Jesus, until our ambition is satisfied and you and we are ONE, for your Name's sake.

AMEN

VAT

I'm not sure if where I want to begin is the best kind of subject for a Monday morning for very many folk. It will hardly be what they would choose to start the day and the week with. It's the subject most folk try to avoid, or get heated about or else it is often the subject of music-hall jokes. Anyhow, I'm going to risk it just for once.

I'm thinking about Tax, the realm of PAYE, SET, capital gains, and now we've got VAT. Not that it's a world I know much about; I have a good friend named Stan who guides me in this maze and anyway I have felt for years that my bit of tax covers the metal polish they must use to keep the brass knocker on Number Ten Downing Street polished and bright, and if so, well that's fair enough and a noble usage. It's really the newcomer, this thing called VAT, that's on my mind. I've heard some very caustic comments about it, like taking with one hand and taking away with the other!

Higher tax for service, but is there always higher service? Well, like it or not, it's there. We've not only got it, we've got it to pay and so we must grin and abide, as the old saying has it. Value Added Tax, the new tax, the most recent tax, and yet I wonder. The more I think about it the more convinced I am that it's the oldest tax in the world, that it's been here since Adam was a lad, as another saying goes. What I'm trying to say is this, that anything at all that has value or worth has a tax, and the greater the value, the greater the worth, the greater is the tax. It's added according to the value; and if that isn't VAT, I don't know what is.

We've always been dog lovers in our house, always had a dog – for odd months from time to time we've even had two. We've valued their faithfulness and affection; but my goodness it's a wrench, a pull, a real sorrow when anything happens to them. There's real grief at losing them. Isn't that a sort of VAT?

You can drop the odd soup bowl you got with coupons

from the petrol station, and who cares? But where it was a love gift, a bit of china given by a dear friend to mark a special occasion, it hurts. Isn't that a bit of VAT too?

Many of the things the thief might take from your house may be covered by insurance. But no insurance can cover the locket that was your mother's, or the watch and chain that was your father's or maybe even your grandfather's. And isn't that VAT again?

You see, in a strange kind of way the tax signifies the value. Now we're getting to the most wonderful truth that I know. The tax, the cost, signifies the value. Well then, when God gave His only begotten Son Jesus to die on a cross, then surely I'm right when I say that no one could pay more dearly than that. But here's the wonder of it; He did it for me, and think of the value and the worth (a better word is the love) He placed on me. VAT, yes; here it is at it's highest and best. He, God, loved me and gave Himself for me.

> *Were the whole realm of nature mine,*
> *That were an offering far too small.*
> *Love so amazing, so divine,*
> *Demands* (I pay my tax) *my soul, my life, my all.*
>
> AMEN

WEST HOUGHTON SUNDAY SCHOOL

For over a decade in our house Top of the Pops, or should I say Top of the Pop-stars has been Cliff Richard. Right from his entry on to the scene he became and remained the idol of my daughter. She had so many photos it saved me the trouble of papering one bedroom for several years. She actually met him once. I think she's only just beginning to get over it. Anyway, he's someone well worth while admiring both as artist and man.

My wife and I were chatting about this late one night and I said we'd not seen or heard of Tom Jones recently, and do you know, the very next day there was an article, an interview with him, in the magazine she takes each week, and I read it.

Fascinating reading it made too. But it was the end bit I liked best of all. I read there these lovely words: 'He's never forgotten his folks', his parents. It went on to tell what he tried to do for them, and at the end Tom Jones said he had a lot to thank his parents for. He went further and said it was due to their upbringing that he had never gone off the rails, for he said they made him what he is today. I hope a whole lot of parents are bothering to read this for I want to ask you quite plainly, how are you bringing up your children?

Oh yes! I know and know only too well in my job as a Methodist minister that all too many have tried to bring up their children well; and their way, the Christian way, has been rejected. But I still believe that we should go on doing this and be sure the fault is never on our side. Not all the geraniums and dahlias we plant bloom fit for Shrewsbury Flower Show in spite of lots of loving care and attention. But that's no reason to pack it all in and shrug your shoulders and say 'who cares anyway?' There are still thousands and thousands, including me, who thank God for a Christian home and upbringing and look back now and know full well we were born into a truly rich family.

I have in my Mission two hostels for boys and well over 90 per cent of those who come under our care come from broken homes or know nothing of a Christian upbringing.

One of my heroes among writers has been for many years Sir Neville Cardus. In one of his books he tells the glorious story of, I think it was, one of the Tyldesley brothers who used to play for Lancashire. Fielding one day at a crucial point in a match, I wonder was it a Roses' match, he seemed to make a catch and the batsman began to walk. The umpire signalled 'out', but Tyldesley said it was no catch – it touched ground first.

Sir Neville complimented him on his piece of honest sportsmanship and subsequently speaking to him he says he asked him why he acted so honestly to the apparent loss of his own team. His reply was this, 'West Houghton Sunday School, tha' knows.'

You see, like Tom Jones, he hadn't forgotten those childhood days and they kept him from going off the rails and stooping to lies and deceit.

I'm sure parents have got a tougher job today in some ways than perhaps they've ever had, but come to think of it they've got the world of tomorrow in their hands. Have you told your youngsters about Jesus, or, what's more important, do they see Him in you?

A prayer to end:

For the gift of children we thank thee. For the way to lead them with our lips and our lives we ask thy help, O Lord.

AMEN

FALSE SUPPOSITIONS

I was about fourteen at the time. My mother was ill in bed with an ear abscess, feeling very poorly. My dad was a railway signalman. He'd gone to work at six a.m. and knocked off at two p.m. so that when I got in from school about four-fifteen p.m., of course he was there. When I walked in he was reclining on the sofa reading his paper, contented as a prince; but I stood at the room door dumbfounded. There he lay quite happy and content, mother upstairs in bed; and there, too, standing in the middle of the hearth rug, was the electric carpet sweeper, switched on and buzzing away like mad. He said, 'Hello!' and I looked at him and walked over and switched off the sweeper. I said, 'What's going on, you left it switched on.' 'Ay lad,' he said, 'switch it on again. It will do your mother far more good than all the doctor's medicine for her, to think the housework isn't being neglected down here. Switch it on again,' and I did. What a man!

My mother lay in bed suffering, not only from an abscess in the middle ear but suffering also from a false supposition.

Well I suppose you could argue that in her case the end justified the means. You could say that what my dad did was plain deception, or you could, I think, call it therapeutic treatment. Indeed, if you'd known my mother as well as I did you would have to admit that my father was right. Still, I must repeat she was suffering from a false supposition.

False suppositions don't always work out like that though, you know. There are times when the consequences are harsh and hard, times when they result in grievous and quite often unnecessary suffering.

I've met folk who supposed that nobody cared for them when the truth was they wouldn't let them.

Then too, there are folk who believe that often what they have done, or maybe left undone, could not possibly be forgiven; when always – always – they could have the forgiveness of Jesus which is so freely offered to all of us, all the time.

There are those who suppose, having met one bad Christian, that all Christians are bad. Having met one person of this or that race or colour and finding them unlikeable they suppose they are then justified in labelling whole groups, indeed whole nations with the same label and suppose them to be all the same, all as bad.

There are those who suppose that what they do doesn't matter. It's their own thing, they can please themselves, they don't want to be reminded that no man is an island.

Others think that what they believe doesn't matter. They suppose it is of no import, yet in the end they do become a someone who is really less than a person.

We need to be aware of our suppositions. They can be right, but my word, they can so easily be wrong.

I'm supposing that Jesus loves me and His promises are faithful and sure. I've tried it for a long time now and it's never been proved to me to be a false supposition. On the contrary, I know it to be gloriously true.

A prayer to end.

Lord Jesus, preserve us from all the ills that follow upon false suppositions and help us to believe in you and your love.

AMEN

FOLLOWING DEAR OLD DAD

It's my son's birthday today and it started me thinking. Nobody has a better son and even when I hear you say that I am biassed, I say, 'yes I am, towards the truth.' It started me thinking about fathers.

We frequently use the expression, 'proud father', and my goodness I've seen a few at the child's baptism in my years as a minister. They look at their offspring as though nobody else had ever had a baby like theirs, and why shouldn't they because nobody else ever has.

Down the years quite naturally I've had easy access into hundreds of homes, been welcomed as a minister and in those grand days before most folk sat in the semi dark and greeted you with 'Sh, Sh,' and continued to glare on at the box, one of the main topics of conversation was the family, and rightly so. Fathers are a bit late in getting off the mark, not well enough versed at the beginning to speak of weighing 12lbs 7ozs, nappy rash and thrush. But when the child talks and walks, says 'Dada' and pulls his hair, then it begins and goes on – started school, got a star, moved into Juniors, eleven plus, O levels, A levels, college, university, engaged, wed, he's a grandfather (the father, not the child I mean).

Well, I think all that is fine and I've said it because it was my own experience. But is all that enough? Weight, health, growth, ability, scholarship, marriage, family – is it enough? Many fathers have done all in their power to encourage all these things, many fathers have made and are making great sacrifices to give their children a better start, a better chance than they themselves had. Many have every reason to be proud of their children's development, achievements and even scholarship and wealth. Grand; but I've lived long enough now to know for sure that none of these things put together necessarily lead to true happiness, to living life with a capital L. You can be clever and selfish, wealthy and unbearable to live with, in a fine house and yet morally in a fine mess.

In the end I'm not too sure if children, our children, your children, bother a great deal about what we say first of all. It's what we are that matters. I'm having the thrill of watching my grandchildren grow up and I know now more than I ever realised before, that above everything children are great copiers, and they copy their idols, and so very, very often that means Dad. I've heard folk say, 'My word, he's like his Dad' about somebody's child; and I've thought, 'My goodness, I hope they only mean in looks.' Who wants to be a chip off the old block if the old block is sour and rotten? Who wants to follow his father's footsteps if he isn't a dear old Dad, but an arrogant, selfish, decadent tyrant? Do you want your lad to be you all over again as you ponder on it in the deep and honest recesses of your own heart?

Jesus once said that He and His Father were one. Are you and your son? You are when you both love and try to follow Jesus.

So we who are fathers pray:

Bless our children and continue to bless us, that in us they may see you.

AMEN

HAMLET – WITHOUT HAMLET

Among other things Christmas time is story time. I can only tell you the story today and you will have to decide for yourself whether or not it is true.

It all happened when I got off the train. Nothing unusual about that, I'd done it umpteen times before, yet this time it was different. For the first time in my life the station master wasn't there. Funny, I thought, perhaps he's ill. Anyway, there was old Fred the porter, he'll soon be retiring, I thought.

'Hello Fred,' I said, 'how's things?'

'All right,' he said.

'Where's the gaffer?' I asked him.

He hung his head in silence. I feared the worst, the old boy must have died, I thought.

'Oh dear me, oh dear me,' Fred said. 'Don't ask, don't ask,' and then out it all came in Fred's own words.

'Maybe you wouldn't know, but the gaffer was due for retirement this year, and when we realised this a few of us thought we ought to do something about it, like, to mark the occasion. You know the old man started work here as a telephone lad in yonder signal box fifty years ago last month. He worked his way up as porter, yard foreman, inspector and then for the last seventeen years he's been station gaffer, and no finer gaffer ever wore our uniform on this or any other railway.

'Well, as I say, we thought we would give him a right proper do and we started a collection and by gum we had a grand response. Enough to give him not only a greenhouse but also an easy chair from passengers and staff. "Champion," we said. "Now when shall we give it to him?"

'In the end we booked the Legion Hall and arranged both a feed and a concert, silver band, conjuror, three soloists and an elocutionist. No written invitations were sent out. It was all hush hush and done by word of mouth lest gaffer should hear a whisper. Oh, and they were coming down from Head Office to make the presentation and to show their esteem.

'The great day came and the do was timed for seven thirty p.m. I went down to the hall early to see if everything was all ready and it was; a lovely spread and all the artists there and a full house. It was time to begin and somebody said, "Where's gaffer?"

'Well, we gave him a minute or two, but when it got quarter to eight there was still no gaffer. Then it dawned on me I'd made all the plans, all the secret preparations down to the last detail, and kept it all dark so to speak, so dark that I'd never told the gaffer to come. I rushed down to his cottage, but the neighbour said his brother-in-law had called for him in his car and taken him to Fordwin, eleven miles away, to a fisherman's dinner there.

'Just fancy, a big do for the gaffer and the gaffer, the honoured guest, wasn't there.'

Ay, and just fancy, Christmas, the feast to celebrate the birthday of Jesus, and Jesus not there!

Well, will He be the honoured guest at your Christmas celebrations?

Now a prayer.

May you, Lord Jesus, be a present and living Lord in our hearts and homes at Christmas.

AMEN

ST MARY WOOLNOTH

Through an amazing combination of circumstances I was preaching recently in an old thirteenth-century church in the City of London in the presence of the Lord Mayor and Lady Mayoress of London and the Sheriff and also to a congregation of American bankers. I began by telling them that in preparing what I had to say I had thought hard and long on what possible connections I had or had had with the City of London and banking. The only link I came across and which perhaps drew us closer together that morning opposite the Bank of England, went back to where I was born in Cheshire.

The slender link was this: just around the corner from where I spent most of my early days, there was a house with a plaque on the outside front wall. On this plaque it stated that Lord Bradbury of Winsford was born there. Now in case you don't know, Lord Bradbury was one time Chief Cashier of the Bank of England and his signature used to be on every pound note; indeed, there was a time when pound notes were commonly referred to as Bradburys.

When I was a schoolboy this same Lord Bradbury was invited to open a church bazaar and naturally there were great preparations for the return of this local boy made good. Banners, bunting and bands were arranged and I'm sure we were given a holiday from school and a fitting and proper deputation was to await his lordship's arrival at the railway station. But small town though it was, Winsford boasted three railway stations in those days. Yes, you've guessed. His lordship turned up at the wrong station. However it all worked out well in the end and he did open the said bazaar.

I like to remember that when the Lord of Glory first visited this earth as a human being He did just that. He turned up at the unexpected place. After all, you don't expect God to be born of an engaged girl whose man is only a carpenter and then go and have the child in a sort of hole in the wall cattle shelter. The King of Kings, God Incarnate, should be born in a palace. He deserves the highest, the best, splendour, pomp and panoply; not a smelly stable, and certainly not in Bethlehem, least of all the possible places. Well, as I say, you just don't expect that sort of thing from THE Lord, do you?

There are far too many folk who still think like that, but even if they don't expect God to turn up like that, that's exactly what He did do that first Christmas that ever was. It was His Majesty the baby, but the cradle was a stall.

I know that as I get ready for Christmas (and I don't mean presents, parcels, pudding and pies), as I get ready to receive the Lord Jesus, I know that again He will come in all humility, to ordinary folk in ordinary homes and bring His extraordinary love and His peace and salvation. Kings and wise men may still come to Him but He comes to all men and only with His coming is Christmas really Christmas. I look at so many lost and lone and sinful folk and as Christmas draws nearer I'm glad, so glad that my Lord and theirs still turns up in unexpected places.

So a prayer to end.

Eternal God, King of Kings and Lord of Lords, guide us as we prepare for your coming at Christmas, coming as a King who laid His glory by and became what we are so that we could become what He is.

AMEN

BROTHER ASS

I've always had a sort of sneaking affection for donkeys, only the four-legged variety mind you, but in spite of their sometimes being stupid my heart always warms to them. The donkey figured in the life of Jesus, you may remember.

At our Mission Farm Home in Essex we have one or two and the baby one that came some months ago was adorable, in fact still is. Before I came to live in London I knew a man in the east midlands who had a donkey. He ran around in a kind of paddock and ran like a Derby winner for a crust or a carrot hung as bait over the gate. When the weather got colder at nights my namesake who owned him brought him in out of the fields for the winter. He stabled him in an out-building. When he fed him in the dark evenings his owner used to switch on the electric light and then every night before going to bed he switched it off.

Going upstairs one night, quite late, he noticed the lighted windows of the building where the donkey was and thought he had forgotten to switch off. He popped on some clothes and ran across and put the light out. Next morning when he got up and went to feed the donkey the light was on again. After a day or so he discovered the donkey was knocking the light switch on with his head. Next night he covered the switch with sticky tape, but the light was on again next morning and the donkey had eaten the tape. He ended up by having to take the bulb out of the lamp-holder. He preferred light to darkness did that donkey.

Have you ever noticed this about the Christmas story? It was while shepherds watched their flock by NIGHT; 'Silent NIGHT, Holy NIGHT'; 'it came upon the MIDNIGHT clear.' It was dark when God laid His glory by and became flesh and dwelt among us. Or, if you doubt the historical detail, it was certainly a dark world into which Jesus came with us to dwell.

My word, there's not a shadow of a doubt that our world is very dark. Wrong is evident, dark and drab and evil things

6

seem to be on the increase. Shadows fall over mankind far round the world, black deeds are done, dark plans are made and more and more familiar lights are being put out. There are those who would go so far as to ask, 'Why celebrate Christmas at all? The very message of peace on earth and reference to men of goodwill has a hollow mocking ring about it in spite of nearly two thousand Christmases past. Can we really be merry and sing and celebrate in this dark world of ours?'

Well I can and I do, no doubt in quite a modest kind of way, but none the less I do, and I'll tell you the reason why.

When St John was writing his version of the Christmas saga he made special reference to the coming of Jesus as the coming of the light of men, and then he wrote this: 'The light shines on in the dark world and the darkness has never put it out.' Now because that's as true today as when it was written, I celebrate the birth of Jesus with as much gladness as those men of old, for He comes again to our dark world to wherever He can find a humble heart wherein to dwell. Even the donkey prefers LIGHT.

My prayer for all of you and yours and me and mine at Christmas is this:

Christ of Bethlehem, be born anew in all our hearts and all our homes.

AMEN

NEW YEAR'S EVE

My mother used to tell me, as a lad, to go and stand on the river bridge on the last day of the year, and I would see a man with as many noses on his face as there are days of the year!

The only New Year resolution I have made now for many years has been the resolution not to make any, which is I reckon, only a cowardly way of getting out of breaking them which so many of us find it all too easy to do.

I think, however, if I was pushed I would covet amongst other things for you and for me that as far as it lay in our power we would always aim at the very best and would not put up with second best, at any rate not in those spheres where it really matters. The number seems to grow all too rapidly of folk who seem to strive might and main for something less than the best in these days. This is rather tragic when the first rate is there to hand. The fruit from off great-grandma's hat is not as good a choice as fresh fruit, and surely nobody ought to be taken in for five seconds with paper roses.

But it's not of fruit and flowers that I'm thinking, except to go on from there to say that real sweetness and abiding quality and perpetual ecstasy only belongs to the true and good. To put it no higher for the moment, nothing is so drab and boring in the end as evil. All too frequently we are taken in by the sham, the veneer, the glitter and gloss of things that are nasty and cheap and shoddy. After all, it's the day of the glossy pictures, the shimmering advert, the spectacular claims, the dazzling sales talk. To bring what I'm saying right down to earth as I like to do, those motor cars on display at the motor show draped with a partially nude female don't go any better or any further with no petrol in these difficult days than a very ordinary, simple and well cared for MOT tested four or five year old banger. And apart from that, no amount of chrome makes up for an empty tank.

Over the years I kept meeting people who had a sort of pity for those of us who are trying to follow Jesus, as though they felt we were deprived, or handicapped or suffering in some way. Oh! if only they could know what I know about the joy that Jesus brings, how freely it is given and how impossible it is for it to be destroyed, apart of course from my own folly. I've found that when I needed pity it was always when I had chosen less than the best, less than Jesus Christ and His way. Or to put it another way, it was when I pleased myself, chose to go my way instead of His and slipped into sham and make-believe and second best mediocrity.

Whatever particular problem comes to your mind as you think of our world, be it war, hunger, anarchy, chaos, industrial strife, broken relationships, crime, disease, squalor, poverty, they all have their roots in the hearts of men who have chosen second best. The very root of the word for SIN in the New Testament is 'missing the mark', not hitting the bull's eye, something less than the highest possible; and yes, I say it again, the root of all our trouble is SIN. There's only one answer to that, the answer is a Saviour – Jesus – and I want Him to be our choice always.

A prayer to end.

Lord Jesus Christ, who didst choose us as the objects of your love and salvation, may our response to that be that we shall always choose you.

AMEN

BOB'S NEW SUIT

You can't even begin to know what a joy it is to speak another word for Jesus, especially at Easter time.

I once told you about my friend Bob and his great faith knowing that he was going to die. Well, he died in the middle of last year, or as our friends in the Salvation Army say, he was 'promoted to glory'. I'll bet he was thrilled to bits when Sunderland got to Wembley.* He grew up in those grey depression years and knew a bit about hardship. Many things that most folk now regard as commonplace rarely came his way. For example, it wasn't often he got a new suit, but when he did he told me (he never told me why) it was always at Easter time. Whenever Easter time came round he always associated it with a new suit. The real significance of this for him only came years later when he became a Methodist minister. It is usual at a funeral for the minister to read these words, 'When this corruptible shall have put on incorruption and this mortal shall have put on immortality . . .'

Less and less people today know what that means; a modern Bible translation makes it a bit plainer: 'when our mortality has been *clothed with immortality*'. Yet even that isn't too plain to too many folk.

But it was clear as daylight to Bob; for him it simply meant that he'd get a new suit when he died and, Hallelujah, he has.

Let me tell you what this means for you and for me too.

It means that Easter isn't just a bank holiday and hot cross buns and a Good Friday ball; that its more than daffodils and lilies. Yes, and its more than early and special Holy Communions and the keeping up of an annual nodding acquaintance with God. It means that Jesus rose from the dead and He's alive, and He promised that because death was not a dam but a door to a new life for Him, it can be like that for us as well, because Jesus the Conqueror reigns

* This talk was given on December 17th, 1973.

and He shall reign for ever and ever. My Saviour and Friend and yours.

I once read a book by a great Scottish preacher of former years and in it he wrote about what he thought was wrong with the Church. He wrote this: 'We (that is, the Church) all too often seem to be living on the wrong side of Easter.' If it's true it's very sad, for this side of Easter is the place of victory and conquest for the followers of Jesus. We're on the winning side, we're sure of a new suit.

Let's end with a prayer.

Thank you, Lord Jesus, for our Easters and the glorious reminder that all who love you will never die.

AMEN

WHIT! WHAT?

All my life what the Church calls Whitsuntide has tended to be, even within the Church, the kind of Cinderella of the Christian festivals. In the north west of this country where I grew up it was almost overlooked, or perhaps smothered would be a better word, smothered beneath Sunday school anniversaries and Whit walks. Could it be that we are reaping what we have sown? Not reaping what we have not sown could be an explanation nearer the truth.

Amongst other things Whitsuntide is the time to remember the fact that God has given power to all His friends, power that never ends. If you do neglect that, and I am suggesting we have, then what follows is weakness and that we most surely have. I'm really glad that on my present motor car there is a switch that is marked 'Reserve petrol'. You see, I've been stranded, temporarily at any rate, for a time on odd occasions when I've neglected the power supply and forgotten to refill. My condition then was not just weakness, it was rather more like death because there was no movement or life at all. Now it's very easy to flick the reserve switch and there's power again and away I go. Renewed power is to hand.

Over the years I have quite often heard good folk pray and they have asked God to send the Holy Spirit to send power to the Church, or maybe to them as individuals. But there is no need to do that, you don't have to ask for what you've already got. Whitsuntide is the time to remember that God has sent His Holy Spirit into the world; the power is here at hand, as handy as a switch as it were. I don't keep striking matches or even lighting a paraffin lamp to read by when it goes dark. I touch the switch and the power in the form of light floods around me.

I know it's a Do-it-Yourself age and a time when more and more folk claim the right to do their own thing, but I know too that it is a sin-sick world we live in. Many, many people live powerless lives, the Church is only ticking over rather than driving onward and upward. Whitsuntide is a reminder of our handy and rightful heritage. It offers us a source of stronger faith, firmer hope and deeper love. Pentecost is not just something which happened to them yonder. It is for us here and now.

A prayer to end.

Spirit of the living God, fall afresh on us.

AMEN

It all happened over ten years ago now but I had a bit of a shock, I recall, at the time. It was one of those occasions when the answer you get to a simple straightforward question is as far removed from anything you might have expected as an Eskimo from the equator.

Let me tell you how it all happened. This chap I know had a fish and chip shop – a good one too, and I was a good patron. He decided to go on a cruise, he and his wife, and off they went and sailed around the Mediterranean. Before he went he showed me the itinerary, and I read it one lunch time over plaice and sixpennyworth and a few peas. My word, it was full of interest, romance, history and sunshine.

Well, away he went – if I remember aright it was for fifteen days in all. He'd been back a week when I next had a chance to chat with him. He was full of it – he could hardly stop for breath as he recited where they had been and what they had seen and he had some grand photographs too to augment the saga. Well, I let him go on for a while because he was enjoying it even more than I was, I think.

But after a time when he paused for breath I said, 'Tell me, when, what was the highlight of it all? What bit meant most to you? What gave you the biggest thrill of all?'

He didn't answer right away but he smiled and nodded to himself and then he said, 'It was on the second Sunday afternoon; yes, that's when it was.'

'What was?' I asked him.

'The biggest thrill of all – you see I rang up home, from the ship mind you, and spoke to our Lilian.'

'Our Lilian' was his daughter he'd left behind at home. You see, apart from the lovely and simple fact that he was missing her there was also the wonder and amazement that from mid-Mediterranean he could get through to her direct and he knew that no matter where he was, if he wished it he could be in constant touch. Any of us who are separated from our families know something of what that means if we and they happen to be on the telephone – STD and we're straight through.

After Jesus was killed and then came back from the dead, and before He left His disciples finally He made them a promise and He gave them His word that He would never really leave them at all, that He would always be available. He said, 'I will not leave you comfortless, there need never be a time when I am not alongside you.' The weekend in the Church Calendar called Whitsuntide, or Pentecost, is when we celebrate the keeping of that previous promise. It's the time when we recall that God the Holy Spirit is living today and is available always to all men. The lines are never all engaged; there's no need to call an operator and you will not be cut off, for the same Jesus said, 'Lo! I am with you always, even to the end of the world.'

Now a prayer.

Holy Spirit of God, make us ever aware of your living and loving presence in all our lives, all the time.

AMEN

THREE IN ONE

A fellow I heard about got married and on their first evening as man and wife it was more than obvious to the bride that her new husband was a very worried man. After some persuasion he confessed he was worried, and all because he felt there was something he should have told her before they got married and he had kept putting it off. He said he could keep it to himself no longer and he confessed and said, 'I'm a somnambulist!'

'Oh!' she replied, 'don't let that worry you; I'm a Baptist – we'll go to your place in the morning and mine in the evening.'

Well I want to make a confession and tell you I'm a Trinitarian. For me this is one of the most difficult things in my faith to explain but I'm going to have a shot at it.

The second home I lived in was in School Road and that house had a claim to fame for it was the first house in that road to go electric. Originally gas lit, we went on the mains. I can well remember as a boy the men digging a trench from the footpath up the side of our house and laying a cable which came up in the house under the cupboard by the fireplace. In that cable there were just two wires, and yet once they were in our house we used them. The same two wires provided lights in every room and lobby and landing, provided heat from electric fires or cooker and provided power to drive the sweeper. The same two wires but with three facets or uses all complementary and making one whole thing, called domestic electricity.

This has always been a help to me in trying to understand the Trinity, to have some idea of what I mean when I read about God who is three in one and also one in three, Father, Son and Holy Spirit, blessed Trinity.

What wonderful riches are mine because I'm a Trinitarian. God is an all-powerful Creator. All I know and all I don't know was made by Him, all the vastness of space is His front garden and He gave the mind and intellect and vision and courage to those who are beginning to explore it. Yet at the same time He is a loving Heavenly Father who above all loved His only Son, and yet gave Him for me and my well-being both now and here, and then yonder. In that Son He became what I am just so that I could become what He is. And to help me along that uphill road, He gave also His Spirit, God with me as I speak, indwelling my life to guard and guide me. He, God the Holy Spirit, walks with me and He talks with me day by day.

Yes, because I'm a Trinitarian God's light is shed on my way, God's love in Jesus warms my heart and God's power through His Holy Spirit is mine always.

I'll end with the Grace:

The Grace of our Lord Jesus Christ, the love of God and the fellowship of the Holy Spirit be with us all evermore.

AMEN

BANK HOLIDAY

I wonder how you spend your Bank Holidays. A major clean and overhaul for the car, a day at the sea or in the country, painting the house, do-it-yourself jobs in the home, visiting, idling, and indeed for very many, working just the same. Well, whatever you plan I'm pleading now for you to try an experiment with me. I want you to give a holiday as well as to have one. Give a holiday to harsh judgements, carping criticisms, seeing the worst. Let me try and show you how it works.

Second to cricket, I've been a football supporter all my life. I'm unashamedly a Wolves' fan. I followed them regularly in those halcyon days when my good friend Stan Cullis was manager. I've been sorry therefore to see the decline in so many ways on the football scene – hooliganism, graft, gamesmanship, big money for little effort – and I've said my share of criticism. But that is NOT all the picture, there's far more on the other side.

In only the last few weeks a few incidents have warmed my heart. A spectator threw a red scarf to Bill Shankly when Liverpool won the League and an official flicked it away with his stick. But Mr Shankly was a big enough man to pick it up and wear it. An Arsenal player got very heated about a certain incident and was obviously voicing his opinion loudly when Bobby Moore of West Ham put an arm round him and covered his mouth for a second or two and then both were laughing and perhaps bookings and fines were prevented and the game went on uninterrupted.

A reporter in a great national newspaper was writing about a Manchester United game and he was glad, as indeed I was, that that great club was not to be relegated. He saw signs of better days, hopes of rebirth, a come back for the team once crippled at Munich. The writer longed for another, shall we say Charlton/Busby era. And then, and this delighted me in modern press coverage, he made a plea for a clean-up of the language and singing on the terraces.

Well, those are some of the good things I've found in the realm of football. So next bank holiday, give yourself a real treat by looking for the good and the best in people, in incidents.

It means a great deal to me to know that Jesus is always looking for and seeing the best in me. He's never harping on the rotten things, but seeking and encouraging the good. There would be no hope for me either here or hereafter if this were not so but *it is*. Let us then be like Jesus. Follow Him, after all He left us an example the Bible says, and look only for the best.

A prayer now:

Bless us all and make our bank holidays memorable because we looked for and found only good things and good folk.

AMEN

GOOD PASTURES

On a Bank Holiday Monday – what do you do? How do you plan to spend it? Do you join the queues on the road? If so, be patient. Do you prefer to miss all that and have a good day in the garden or installing a 'do-it-yourself' wardrobe? Or are you one of those who still have to work, bank holiday or no bank holiday, so that others can enjoy themselves.

We were talking recently in my home about how we used to spend bank holidays as youngsters. As a rule we went into the fields amidst the grass and the pastures, the woods and streams, the wild flowers and birds. Happy days, never over-crowded and all free too!

As someone who grew up in the lovely dairy county of Cheshire (is it still there or have we messed about with that? I don't think so), I know a bit about fields and pastures. An oak tree fairly near my old home marks the middle of Cheshire according to the plaque on it.

But now I want to switch to the seaside, for a lot of you will be off there for the holiday, I reckon. A few weeks ago I went for the first time to Southend-on-Sea. In the vestry there they have got the same custom they had in my last church, before I came to Whitechapel. At the end of their minister's stay with them, they hang him in the vestry – fitly framed, of course. In this vestry at Southend there they were, ten or a dozen of them. The first one was of a Methodist minister named A. E. Whitham and I was so delighted because one of his books made a great impression on me when I was a Methodist local preacher in my teens. It was called *In the Pastures of His Presence* and the 'His' was Jesus, and the sub-title said it had to do with the culture and discipline of the spiritual life.

It's good and right to have a special holiday to refresh our bodies and minds with a break from work. But are you really bothering much about feeding your spiritual life, about feeding in the pastures of the Presence of Jesus? He said He was the Good Shepherd – we are His sheep. Do we do much grazing in our Shepherd's pastures, I wonder? There are many ways and many places to do this. I have only time to mention one, but it's a very rich pasture and all too often neglected. Indeed, I find it one of the easiest and commonest things to put off for other things – albeit other good things.

I'm thinking of that pasture called prayer. This is the place where saints, apostles, prophets and martyrs have fed. I would go so far as to say no one has ever done anything of any real import for Jesus Christ's sake who hasn't fed long and often in this pasture. It is the power-house, the filling-station, the place of repair and renewal – there the tuning up is done and the drive is given and reliability is ensured. Well, have a good bank holiday whether you're playing at home or away. I wish you journeying mercies if you intend to travel and may the day's end have brought you nothing but joy. But give a bit of time and thought to making steadfast plans to feed your soul in the presence of Jesus.

A prayer for us all:

Grant us a blessed day O Lord and keep alive within us an appetite for the fulness of joy which you have to give us.

AMEN

JOHN JACKSON HAS ALSO WRITTEN
IT WAS ON A MONDAY MORNING
published by Lakeland paperbacks